A SMALL BUSINESS GUIDE TO DIRECT MAIL

A SMALL BUSINESS GUIDE TO DIRECT MAIL

Build your customer base and boost profits

Lin Grensing

Self-Counsel Press
(a division of)
International Self-Counsel Press Ltd.
Canada   U.S.A.
Printed in Canada

Printed in Canada

First edition: November, 1991

Canadian Cataloguing in Publication Data
Grensing, Lin, 1959-
        A small business guide to direct mail
(Self-counsel business series)
ISBN 0-88908-976-0

        1. Advertising, Direct-mail — United States.
2. Advertising, Direct-mail — Canada. I.Title.
II. Series.
HF5861.G73   1991   659.13'3   C91-091750-7

Self-Counsel Press
(a division of)
International Self-Counsel Press Ltd.
Head and Editorial Office
1481 Charlotte Road
North Vancouver, British Columbia V7J 1H1

U.S. Address
1704 N. State Street
Bellingham, Washington 98225

CONTENTS

SAMPLES

TABLES

INTRODUCTION

Direct mail was the shining star of advertising in the 1980s and promises to continue to be so in the 1990s. It's the fastest growing form of advertising because it's measurable, relatively easy to produce, and cost effective.

When you run a radio spot for your product or service it's hard to tell exactly how effective it was. When you mail a coupon to prospective customers, however, it's easy to measure the results — simply count the coupons you get back.

As direct mail has become more prominent, it has attracted the attention of advertising agencies and direct marketing "gurus" who have attempted to envelope this inherently simple advertising technique in confusing jargon, complicated mathematics, and mystical computer techniques. But direct mail isn't difficult and it's not beyond the means of the average small business owner. It requires —

(a) a strong product,

(b) a clearly identifiable market,

(c) a mailing list to reach that market, and

(d) a mailing package.

It sounds simple enough and it really is. The information in this book will make it easy for you to plan and produce your own direct mail campaign.

With direct mail, your marketing dollars aren't wasted as they might be in other forms of advertising because you're targeting your promotion specifically to those people who will be most interested in your product. Let's take a look at a simple comparison.

You're selling a line of clothing for pregnant women. You could advertise on television — perhaps a spot on a cable network during a program whose audience is primarily women in their childbearing years. The key word here, though, is primarily. Why? Because in addition to these viewers, there will undoubtedly be female viewers in other age groups as well as men and children. Even the women who are in their "childbearing years" may very well not be pregnant (or planning to become pregnant) at the time your commercial is airing. But you're paying to reach all of these viewers. And you are, in effect, throwing a portion of your money away.

If you were using direct mail, however, you could find and purchase a list of women who subscribe to a magazine specifically for pregnant women. Or a list of women who have purchased maternity clothes from another manufacturer. You pay only to reach those people you identify as prime targets for your advertising message.

Most of all, direct mail is growing because it works. One out of two consumers ordered goods from catalogs or by mail order in the past year, according to a survey conducted by Mediamark Research Inc. In case you missed it, that's *50% of all consumers* — nothing to sneeze at. Those could be *your* customers. All you have to do is find them and make the right contact. What could be more direct than that? And *that* is what this book is all about: making direct mail work for your business.

1

WHAT IS DIRECT MAIL?

a. DIRECT MAIL AS DIRECT MARKETING

Direct marketing is marketing that is directed at a specific individual (or, more accurately, a group of individuals) and is intended to elicit an immediate response (e.g., placement of an order or generation of an inquiry).

In fact, the only requirement for a marketing effort to be classified as direct marketing is that the message and the response be direct and immediate. General advertising is designed to convince consumers to make a purchase at some later date. When you watch a commercial for McDonald's, for instance, the people who developed the commercial don't expect you to immediately jump up, get in your car, and buy a burger. Direct marketing, on the other hand, is designed to elicit just such an immediate response.

Direct marketing may use one or more of the following techniques:

(a) Telephone

(b) Television

(c) Space ads

(d) Billboards

(e) Mail

1. Telephone

You're sitting down to eat dinner when the phone rings. You answer it and, to your chagrin, it's one of those telemarketers trying to sell you something. Only this time that "something" is a magazine that you really are interested in and the price is right. You bite. Some clever businessperson used telephone direct marketing to reach right into your home and make a sale.

2. Television

It's late and you can't sleep. The program you're watching is interrupted by a musical performer from days gone by strumming a guitar and promoting an album collection of greatest hits. To order, all you have to do is call a toll-free number now.

Or you're watching what you think is a regular program only to discover that you're in the midst of a long commercial known as an infomercial. The infomercial idea is not new; only the name is. The 30-minute commercial emerged in the 1950s. As programming time became harder and harder to get, the Federal Trade Commission outlawed these commercials. Now, however, with the renaissance of cable networks, they are back on the air in greater abundance than ever.

Infomercials are used to promote products ranging from seminars to cosmetics. One of these half-hour programs, "Love Phone With Jessica Hahn," encourages callers to phone in to speak with "love counselors," for a fee per call, of course.

How far can technology take us? TV Answer Inc. has proposed a two-way interactive television network based on new technology it has developed. This technology would allow consumers to use a home unit box about the size of a VCR for pushbutton ordering of products and services from regular TV programming menus. This is about as direct as direct marketing can get!

3. Space ads

You're flipping through a magazine when your attention is caught by an interesting ad for product XYZ. To order, all you have to do is call a convenient 800 number or clip and mail the attached coupon.

4. Billboards

You're driving to work when you notice a large billboard featuring a ballerina against a black background with a headline that reads simply "1-800-FLOWERS. Anytime, anywhere, to anyone." This is an actual, very successful billboard created by a company called 800-Flowers. The billboards were featured in 588 markets nationwide in January, 1990 (in time for Valentine's Day).

Flowers aren't the only products being direct marketed on billboards. The Schieffelin and Somerset Co. tested direct-response billboards displaying an attractive man or woman with a tag line that read, "My number is ... and I drink Johnnie Walker." The company ended up with hundreds of responses (as many as 400 a day in fact!) A series of holiday billboards rolled out in November, 1989, pictured a reindeer saying, "My number is 1-800-2-SCOTCH. And I'll deliver Johnnie Walker." Five percent of the people who called in placed an order.

5. Mail

You come home from work, reach into your mailbox, and pull out a catalog. A catalog of gift products, of clothing, of cheeses, of just about any grouping of products you can imagine. You bring it inside, leaf through it, make a few choices and either phone in your order to an 800 number or fill out and mail the order form in the catalog.

In direct mail, the mail serves a critical function: it is used as a means of getting a sales message out to qualified prospects and is then, in turn, used by those prospects to place an order or express an interest in receiving additional information.

In *The Complete Direct Mail List Handbook,* Ed Burnett defines direct mail as "a means of promotion delivered exclusively through the ... mails on a one-to-one relationship to induce from the individual recipient direct (and usually immediate) response through the phone or the mail. The desired response can be in the form of a transfer of money (for a purchase, subscription, or contribution), or it can be in the form of a request for additional information or a copy of some proffered promotion in the form of a booklet, pledge or catalog."

6. Pros and cons of direct marketing methods

Telephone direct marketing has the advantages of immediacy and personal interaction with the potential customer, but many people feel telephone marketing is intrusive and will react negatively to a phone call. In addition, some offers are too complex to be explained adequately in a short phone conversation.

Television direct marketing offers the strong impact of both visual and auditory messages at the same time. It is, however, much more expensive than other forms of direct marketing and, although some cable stations now offer marketers the opportunity to target specific market segments, the message will still reach a large number of people who are not likely to be interested in the product.

Space ads can be an inexpensive way of doing direct marketing, and the wide variety of trade and technical publications offers marketers an opportunity to target finite market segments. However, a space ad in a multi-page publication is competing with many other messages (including other ads) for the reader's attention.

Billboards are "larger than life" and thus offer a strong visual impact, particularly in heavy traffic areas. However, because of the short time a driver has to read the message, advertising copy must be kept to a bare minimum. And, as with television, the audience is so varied that it is difficult to target one specific segment.

Direct mail is the king of direct marketing. It offers the marketer the chance to fully explain the product offering and direct the offer to a specifically targeted market, at a fraction of the cost of television or telemarketing campaigns.

b. WHAT CAN YOU SELL THROUGH THE MAIL?

What can you sell through the mail? Just about anything.

Sweeter Measures is a company in Nebraska that sells clothing in sizes 42-72. Clothing is one of the most popular items sold through the mail.

Benihana Restaurants, the famous Japanese steakhouse chain, sells gourmet steaks and lobster tails through the mail. Lobsterline, a St. Paul mail-order company also sells lobster — live lobster that are delivered door to door by Federal Express courier.

Calyx & Corolla is a company in San Francisco that sells exotic fresh flowers through a catalog. Long-stem roses, eucalyptus, lilies, daisies — you name it, they sell it and ship direct from the grower to the customer.

Rotocast Display Products of Miami offers life-size replicas of carousel horses from the turn of the century.

In 1989, *Direct Marketing Magazine* carried a piece about sales of three premium French champagnes through the mail — under the label of the Marquis de Sade Champagne!

The New York Racing Association, with its agency Backer Spielvogel Bates created a $2 million multi-media campaign to boost attendance at the Breeder's Cup. The direct mail piece they created was sent to their database of 160,000 frequent track-goers, compiled by collecting names and addresses through special contests.

Avon Inc., known for its reliance on personal representatives and the familiar "Avon calling!" slogan, is testing a direct marketing program with its Avon Select catalog, mailed to customers whose names have been provided by sales representatives. The catalog features the Avon beauty line and other products.

Even some of the movie studios are using the mail to reach potential movie-goers directly. They've found it less expensive and more targeted than other, more traditional, forms of advertising. Fox launched a direct marketing program to promote its "Miller's Crossing," in a few top metropolitan areas. They sent 150,000 personalized, 10-page, 4-color booklets to upscale Manhattan residents. Warner also used direct mail to market its "Memphis Belle" to several specific markets, including war veterans, high school students, and young women.

c. WILL DIRECT MAIL WORK FOR YOU?

Not everything, however, will prove to be a successful mail-order product. Will your product sell through the mail? Following are five important questions to ask yourself before embarking on a direct mail campaign. If you can answer yes to each of these questions, you're ready to proceed.

1. Can you reach your market effectively through direct mail?

Suppose you're selling a product that appeals to lawyers. It's easy enough to get a list of lawyers. You can reach your market. But, suppose you're selling a product that appeals to 30-year old redheads who collect stamps. You're going to have a very hard time finding a list of these prospects. And, even if you are lucky enough to find a list (of subscribers to the *30-Year-Old Redhead Stamp Collectors' Magazine*, for instance), the number of potential customers will be so small that you won't be able to sell very large quantities of your product. As we'll see when we get into a discussion of mailing lists, in direct mail the list is the most important aspect of your marketing effort. If you can't reach your market (e.g., can't find a list or enough lists), you can't sell your product.

2. Does your product have broad appeal?

Clothing has broad appeal. Everybody wears clothes. Many people buy clothes for fun, or to be fashionable, and these people buy clothes again and again because their old wardrobes become dated, or because they want more fun. Even those who wear clothing strictly for utilitarian purposes need new clothes when theirs wear out. Clothing is also a common gift item.

Candle snuffers, on the other hand, have a very limited appeal. Most people rely on electricity these days, and even those who like to use candles occasionally to set a certain mood probably already own a candle snuffer, (or don't want one). Once you have one candle snuffer, you have enough.

3. Does your product stand out from the crowd?

There are literally hundreds of catalogers who sell clothing through the mail. If you're entering the clothing market, there has to be something about your line of clothing that makes it different from the hundreds of other lines already firmly entrenched in the buyers' minds.

In fact, whatever you're selling needs to have a unique appeal that will make it valuable to potential customers — whether the appeal lies in pricing, quality, or availability.

4. Can you describe your product by mail?

Clothing can be sold readily via mail because it's relatively easy to describe or show via photographs. On the other hand, selling cars or homes through the mail would be very difficult. Why? Because they're extremely complex, quite expensive items that consumers need to know a lot about before they can make a purchase decision — more than you could tell (or show) them in a single mailing.

Similarly, products or services which are very ephemeral can be difficult to sell through the mail — e.g., college enrollment, insurance plans, etc. While mail might play a role in the overall marketing of these services, it won't be the element that "closes the deal," and it won't work alone.

5. Can you make a profit?

If your product sells for less than $15 and it's the only product you've got, you probably won't be able to make enough to support your advertising costs. We'll be taking a more detailed look in chapter 2, section **f.** at how to calculate a break-even point for your mailings and how to maximize your profit margins.

d. WHICH COMES FIRST — THE PRODUCT OR THE MARKET?

Which should you do — develop or discover a product you would like to sell and then search for a market, or find a market with a certain need and develop a product to meet that need?

Without exception, savvy marketers will suggest that you do the latter. Certainly there are success stories of companies that have succeeded by going at it the other way, but your chances of success are much, much higher if you seek to meet an existing need, rather than searching for a market that may or may not exist and trying to convince this market that they have a need they may or may not have.

2

BEHIND THE SCENES: THE HIDDEN WORK IN DIRECT MAIL

What your customers will see of your direct mail is the actual physical piece itself: the letter, the brochure, the envelope, the catalog. But before you begin developing these tangible parts of your direct mail package, there is a lot of "behind the scenes" work that needs to be done and some potential pitfalls to be aware of.

a. IDENTIFYING YOUR OBJECTIVES

Before you can even begin to think about the specifics of your direct mail campaign, you need to determine what your objectives are. You may want to —

(a) develop new markets,

(b) increase awareness of your company name,

(c) secure leads for your sales force, or

(d) increase sales.

Perhaps you're currently selling lawn and garden equipment and would like to add a line of sporting goods or you're running seminars for secretaries and would like to start programs for a management-level audience. In each of these cases, your advertising objective is to develop new markets.

If you're just opening a new business or if you need to differentiate yourself from competitors, you might need to increase awareness of your company name. Direct mail is one way to accomplish this.

If you use a direct sales force for some of your selling, you may want to qualify prospects rather than having your sales-people make cold calls. Direct mail can help you identify people who have an interest in your product or service before you send a salesperson out on the road.

Perhaps the most common objective for direct mailers is simply to increase sales. You want more people to spend more money on your product or service.

There are other objectives and the one you choose will depend on the product or service you're trying to sell. Your objectives may very well change each time you run a new campaign.

It's important, though, that you do identify an objective each time you mail — without it your mailings will not have a focus. In addition, you will have a difficult time measuring results because you won't know what results you were trying to obtain in the first place.

You also need to be very specific when you're establish-ing these goals. You need to outline exactly what you want to do and where you want to go. If your goal is to increase sales, decide by how much — by 25%? by 30%? If your goal is to increase response, by how much? Do you want to increase your response from 1% to 2%? From 0.5% to 1%? By being very specific, you will be able to measure the effective-ness of the advertising you do.

b. ANALYZING YOUR PRODUCT

Of course you know your product, you say. How ridiculous. Who else could know it as well as you do? Your customers, that's who. And, sometimes, they may be seeing benefits to your product that you haven't even considered yet. That's why you need to do your homework. You need to examine your product carefully and answer such questions as the following:

(a) What does it look like? Be specific. If you're selling books, you'll want to consider such things as the books' size, the type of binding, and the size of type (e.g., large, easy-to-read). If you're selling clothing, you'll want to think about the color, the construction, the style. If you're selling office equipment, you'll want to consider the size and details, such as the hardware used (e.g., "finely carved wooden handles," or "sturdy metal pull bars.")

(b) What does it do? A dress or suit does more than cover your body: it "gives you an aura of sophistication" or "looks businesslike but feels like you're wearing your favorite pair of old jeans." Look beyond the obvious, to consider points that are unique to your product and will convey special meaning to your customer.

(c) What is it made of? Can you boast of special materials? Strong materials? Environmentally conscious materials?

(d) What color, texture, size is it? Your customers will want to know details. Remember, your brochure or catalog is your "store." You want to be so specific that your customers feel as though they're standing there in your storeroom looking at and touching your product.

(e) What is its primary use? Don't feel that this is a silly consideration — of course they know that you use a pen to write with, so spell it out. But spell it out with some added allure: "You'll be glad you chose the elegant Micro Pen the next time you're taking notes at an important conference."

(f) What is (or what might be) its secondary use? Does your product have a use other than what you initially intended it for? You can find out by speaking with your customers and being attuned to their feedback. Baking soda, for example, originally intended as a cooking ingredient, is now also advertised as a refrigerator/freezer deodorant.

(g) How much does it cost to manufacture? This is an important question to answer since it will, in part, determine how you will price your product. Don't overlook any element in the cost formula. Obviously, you'll consider raw materials. But also take into account such things as salaries, overhead, and depreciation on equipment.

(h) How much do you charge your customers? Suppose you're selling hand-knit sweaters. You may have one price for standard sizes and a premium price for petite or extra large sizes. You may offer special pricing for quantity purchases or special package offers.

(i) How will your product make the lives of your customers easier? Will your non-skid coffee mug make travelling to work in the morning with a cup of scalding hot coffee less perilous? What will your product do for your customers? How will it make them happier, healthier, or wiser?

(j) How does your product compare to competitive products on the market? Know your competitors. Know your competitors' products. How are they priced? How are they constructed? What do they offer that your products don't? How do they fall short when compared to your products? As a consumer, why would you choose your product instead of someone else's?

(k) Does your product fill a definite need or desire? The most successful new product inventions fill a specific need in the marketplace. 3M's Post-it Notes, for instance, were an immediate success because they offered businesspeople a quick and easy way to write notes and attach them to virtually anything. What need does *your* product fill?

(l) Does it satisfy most current users? Contact with your customers is critical to success in any field. Be a good listener — ask for criticism. Instead of asking customers whether they like your product, ask how your product could be improved. Their comments will provide valuable information that you can use to increase the value of your offerings and identify potential problem areas.

(m) Does it have any exclusive features? If you can claim to be the only one offering something, you have a distinct advantage over competitors. Is there something unique or exclusive to your product? Find it, focus on it, and you'll have customers beating a path to your door.

(n) Is it "positioned" correctly? Am I trying to sell it to the right market? If you feel like you're banging your head against the wall in your attempts to move your product into the marketplace, you may have targeted the wrong market. Step back and reconsider your approach. Who are the people who really need this product? Are there other sub-groups that might also be potential customers? If your current prospects aren't buying, what do you think is the reason? Again, when in doubt, ask your customers. They, not you, are the experts when it comes to your products and their use (and lack of use).

When answering these questions, remember that it's important to be as objective as possible. It's not unusual for a marketer to fall in love with his or her own product. Unfortunately, it's also not unusual for the marketplace to react less than enthusiastically to the introduction of this product.

13

If you feel that you can't be objective enough, solicit the advice of people you trust. These do not have to be "experts," but they should be people you can trust to think seriously and speak honestly about your product. You may even decide to conduct an informal survey.

c. ANALYZING YOUR MARKET

Once you thoroughly understand what it is you're trying to sell, you can turn to the question of who you are trying to sell it to and how best to reach them. Consider these questions:

(a) Who are you trying to reach?

(b) When do you want to reach these customers?

(c) Where do your prospects live?

(d) How often do you want to reach your prospects?

(e) Where do you want to reach potential customers?

1. Who are you trying to reach?

Define your potential customer in terms of both demographic and psychographic characteristics. Demographic characteristics include such things as age, sex, income, education, family status, and occupation. Psychographic characteristics involve lifestyle or attitudes. If you don't know specifically who you're trying to reach, you'll have a very difficult time trying to determine the best list to reach them.

2. When do you want to reach these customers?

If your product is seasonal (e.g., a ski catalog), you will not be mailing in mid-July. Be careful, however, not to reach your customers too late. Your goal is to reach the consumer at the point when the purchasing decision is made — this is not necessarily the same point at which the purchase is made. You may very well find that you need to begin promoting ski gear in October.

3. Where do your prospects live?

Your choice of list will certainly depend on where your prospects live. Perhaps your product has national appeal and you are able to use national lists. This will usually, but not always, be the case.

However, if your product or service is regional — seminars or catalogs of regional foods, for instance — you would not be making effective use of your mailing dollars to mail nationally.

4. How often do you want to reach your prospects?

Will you do regular monthly mailings? Quarterly? It's important to mail your own customer list on a regular basis so you keep your name before them and so you take advantage of the momentum created by a recent purchase. Remember, "your best customers are your best customers." You'll want to mail to them regularly and monitor the response to these mailings closely so you aren't mailing either too often or too infrequently.

5. Where do you want to reach potential customers?

At home? In the office? The type of product or service you provide will determine the best place for reaching prospects. If you were selling a subscription to a trade publication, you would probably want to reach prospects in the office. If you were selling clothing, you would probably want to reach them at home. But this isn't always the case. You may want to test some different approaches just to see what kind of response you get.

Once you've thoroughly analyzed your customers, you need to take a close look at your prospects. Who are you trying to sell this product to? The following questions can help you get a good feel for your audience:

(a) Are your best prospects men or women?

(b) Are they young, middle-aged, or old?

(c) Are they rich, poor, or average?

(d) Where do most of your prospects live?

(e) What are their tastes?

(f) How much do they already know about the product?

Again, if you don't know the answers to these questions, consider sending a short questionnaire to your current customers.

It's extremely important to know who your current customers are. By knowing the characteristics of current customers, you'll have a much easier time of prospecting for new customers because you'll know exactly what to look for when you're researching mailing list availability.

Another important aspect of identifying your market is determining their specific buying habits. When you're considering the purchasing habits of your potential customers, you'll want to know the following information regarding the product you're selling.

(a) Where do customers typically buy this product?

Suppose you're introducing a line of deli foods that you'd like to sell through the mail. Traditionally, customers would buy deli items at a deli. You'll need to address this obvious objection to purchasing through the mail in your advertising materials. In addition, knowing that there are alternative sources of supply will help you in determining pricing, developing unique benefits, and structuring your offer.

(b) Are purchases seasonal or special occasion?

The answer to this question will help you plan your mailing strategy. Obviously, if you're selling Christmas items, you won't be mailing in June; neither would you mail in December, which would be too far into the season. You might, instead, opt for a late October mailing date. Seasonal considerations also apply to swimsuits, educational materials (which often see low sales during summer months), and gardening supplies.

(c) Is purchase premeditated or impulsive?

Direct mail works best for selling impulse items. Premeditated purchases (e.g., cars) lead consumers to local retail outlets. They won't sit around to wait for a brochure to show up in their mailbox.

(d) How does your price compare with competitors'?

Again, pricing is a major consideration, as it forms the basis for your offer. Know who your competitors are — both your direct mail competitors and alternative sources of supply. If a consumer can conveniently buy a very similar item locally at a good price, your direct mail offer may not have much appeal. You'll need to structure an offer that points out the benefits of your pricing, fast delivery, etc., to woo them from more traditional sources of supply.

d. FEATURES VS. BENEFITS

A well-known guideline in the advertising industry is "sell the sizzle, not the steak." If the physical product you want a consumer to purchase is a razor, what you may really be selling is a smooth shave. In fact, it's most often what the product will do for the consumer (or what they perceive it will do) that you're selling, not the product itself. If your product is cosmetics, you're really selling a smooth, wrinkle-free complexion. If your product is a diet aid, you're really selling a trim body.

Very few consumers care about how your product is manufactured. What they care about is what it will do for them. Yet many advertisers spend a great deal of advertising dollars telling potential customers how their product is made, explaining the *features* of what they have to offer instead of the *benefits*.

17

The difference between a feature and a benefit is a troubling distinction to many involved in the field of direct mail or the broader field of advertising. Yet this distinction is fundamental to the trade. It's the point at which your product and your market meet.

A feature is some aspect of your product that is important to its salability — price, color, materials, etc.

A benefit is what the customer gets out of the product or service and its features. If the feature is "Made with extra-strength Suprasteel," the benefit might be "Eliminates the cost and bother of annual replacements."

You probably already know what the features of your product or service are. To determine what kind of benefits they add up to, simply ask the pertinent question from the customer's point of view: "What does that mean to *me*?" The answer will be a benefit.

For instance, you might think of saying in an ad: "*The Management Book* has information on how to manage employees." This, however, is only a feature. So, now ask, from the customer's point of view, "What does that mean to *me*?" Answer (and benefit): "You'll be able to find countless tips that you can immediately apply to the employees you manage — your job will be easier, your department will be more productive, you'll be more promotable."

When you plan your advertising, look for the benefits of your product or service. Put yourself in the consumer's place and ask the questions, "What's in it for me?" "How will my life be made easier by purchasing this product?"

e. FINDING YOUR USP

Another important aspect of searching for benefits is finding your USP — or *unique selling proposition*. What sets your product apart from all others? What one unique feature do you have that nobody else has? Do you manufacture the only pen that will write at any angle? The only pizza that's sold through the mail? The only tools with a lifetime guarantee?

You need to create awareness of your product or service by differentiating it from similar products or services available to your customers.

Maybe you'll need to do a great deal of brainstorming to come up with something that sets you apart. But, once you find it, be assured that you have a powerful advertising tool that you can use in all of your mailings.

What if your product has no USP? It happens. But there are still some things you can do to make your mailings memorable. For instance:

- Use an actual person as a spokesperson.

- Invent a trademark character.

- Use an unforgettable theme line.

- Use unique mailing packages.

f. THE MAGICAL BREAK-EVEN POINT

It doesn't take a financial wizard to figure out that the best way to determine whether it makes sense to conduct a particular kind of marketing activity is to determine the break-even point, the point at which the money you spend and the money you make are the same. This is the point you need to achieve before you start realizing profits. Any point below this level means that you suffer a loss.

When you do a mailing, you need to know how many orders you will have to generate to cover all of the costs of that mailing. That point is the break-even point.

The "Break-even Analysis Form" (see Sample #1) is an example of how you can use a simple spreadsheet program to forecast revenue, calculate break-even point, and adjust expenses to review the implication of various mailing options.

The figures on the form are used for comparative purposes only and don't necessarily represent actual costs.

The first step in completing this form is to fill in the top section with the date, name of your product, and retail price of the product (for simplicity, we will be using only the retail price in calculations but you may have a number of different price points that you need to consider).

This form is broken down into three areas:

- fixed costs (your direct-mail costs),

- variable costs (your product and fulfillment costs), and

- margin (a calculation of break-even units and the percent return required from your mailing to reach this break-even point).

1. Fixed costs

Your fixed costs will include the cost of any mailings or other advertising you will be doing to promote your product. While this form only includes the costs of various mailings, you could also add lines for other advertising you're doing, for example space advertising. You could have as few or as many line items as you need to plan your promotional campaign. For each list, you would need to fill in the following columns:

(a) *List:* What list will you be using? Include a descriptive title here that will make it easy for you to identify the list later.

(b) *# Mld:* How many labels from this list segment do you plan to mail?

(c) *CPM:* What is the cost per thousand of the list you will be using? Be sure to include costs for any selections or key coding you will request.

SAMPLE #1
BREAK-EVEN ANALYSIS FORM

```
 1      A       B       C       D       E        F        G       H     I       J
 2  BREAKEVEN ANALYSIS FORM
 3  Date:
 4  Product:
 5  Retail Price  $75.00
 6  --------------------------------------------------------------------------------
 7  FIXED COSTS (DIRECT MAIL)
 8                          LIST   PRINTING POSTAGE          PROJ.           %
 9  LIST      # MLD   CPM   COST    COST    COST  CREATIVE  SALES  REV.   RETURN
10
11  House File  5000   0.00    0.00  750.00  945.00  2000.00    67  5000.00  1.00
12  Compiled #1 5000  30.00  150.00  750.00  945.00             67  5000.00  1.00
13  Compiled #2 5000  30.00  150.00  750.00  945.00             67  5000.00  1.00
14  Compiled #3 5000  30.00  150.00  750.00  945.00             67  5000.00  1.00
15  Respondent # 5000 75.00  375.00  750.00  945.00             67  5000.00  1.00
16  Respondent # 5000 75.00  375.00  750.00  945.00             67  5000.00  1.00
17  Respondent # 5000 75.00  375.00  750.00  945.00             67  5000.00  1.00
18  Respondent # 5000 75.00  375.00  750.00  945.00             67  5000.00  1.00
19
20    Totals  40000 390.00 1950.00 6000.00 7560.00 2000.00   533 40000.00  1.00
21  --------------------------------------------------------------------------------
22  VARIABLE COSTS (PRODUCT/FULFILLMENT)
23
24                 Per Unit
25  Unit Product     15.55                                       8293.33
26  Unit Fulfillment  5.75                                       3066.67
27  Royalty @ 12%     9.00                                       4800.00
28  Other             2.25                                       1200.00
29
30                              Total Variable Costs   17360.00
31  --------------------------------------------------------------------------------
32  CALCULATION OF MARGIN
33
34  Total Unit Sales:                                     533
35  Total Fixed Costs:                                17510.00
36  Total Var. Costs:                                 17360.00
37  Total Revenue:                                    40000.00
38  Breakeven Units:                                      465
39  % Return:                                           1.16%
40  $ Margin:                                          5130.00
41  --------------------------------------------------------------------------------
42  COMMENTS:
43
44
45
49
50
51
52
53
54
55
56
57
58
59
```

(d) *Printing cost:* The printing cost is calculated on a formula that you can adjust to represent your own cost per piece mailed. In this case, a cost of 15¢ per piece was used.

(e) *Postage cost:* The postage cost is also calculated on a formula. In this case a cost of 18.9¢ was used.

(f) *Creative:* Here you would include the total cost of any creative services required to prepare your package (e.g., copy, design, or photography).

(g) *% return:* In this column you would include the % return you anticipate from each list you will be mailing. If this is the first mailing you will be doing, you will have to make an educated guess at the return. If you have past history from previous mailings, you can use this to estimate the response you might receive. In Sample #1, a figure of 1% was used for each of the lists mailed.

Once this information has been filled in, the program will calculate your projected sales and revenue based on the numbers you've used.

2. Variable costs

Variable costs are those costs that depend on the response to your mailings. For instance, if you receive 10 orders, your product costs will only need to take into account the cost of 10 products. If you receive 100 orders, you will need to calculate your cost for 100 products. Thus, this is a variable measure.

In this section you need to fill in the per unit cost for your product, fulfillment of orders, royalties, or any other miscellaneous cost associated with the product you're selling.

The worksheet will then calculate your total variable costs using the "projected sales" calculated under section 1.

3. Margin

This section is calculated based on the information you provided under sections 1 and 2. Here you'll find that your break-even point is 465 units, which requires an overall 1.16% return, and your total margin is $5130.

4. Adjusting the figures

The beauty of a spreadsheet is that you can "play with" the numbers. Suppose you decide that a 1.16% return is too high. You don't think you'll do that well on this, perhaps your first, mailing. You need to adjust your costs so that you can break-even at a lower percent return.

To do this, simply return to the top of the worksheet and review the costs you can control. For instance, you might decide that you can't afford to use respondent lists at $75/m or that you need to cut down the number of pieces you're mailing. Perhaps you decide that your creative costs are too high or that you need to trim your product costs. Simply make these adjustments on the form to see how that affects your break-even point.

Samples #2, #3, #4, and #5 show the effect on the bottom line of making various changes to the first form. Sample #6 provides the formulas used to create this worksheet.

g. THE KEYS TO A SUCCESSFUL CAMPAIGN

In the chapters ahead, we will look more specifically at the steps involved in developing a direct mail package. However, first let's look at the keys to a powerful direct mail campaign.

1. Have a specific goal in mind

If you settle for a broad objective like "increase sales" you won't be able to accurately measure the effectiveness of your advertising. You need to choose a specific, quantifiable goal that will later help you to measure results.

```
1    A        B      C      D      E       F       G        H      I        J
2   BREAKEVEN ANALYSIS FORM
3   Date:
4   Product:
5   Retail Price  $85.00
6   -------------------------------------------------------------------------
7   FIXED COSTS (DIRECT MAIL)
8                              LIST   PRINTING POSTAGE          PROJ.          %
9   LIST        # MLD   CPM    COST   COST     COST   CREATIVE  SALES  REV.   RETURN
10
11  House File  5000    0.00   0.00   750.00   945.00 2000.00    59  5000.00  1.00
12  Compiled #1 5000   30.00  150.00  750.00   945.00             59  5000.00  1.00
13  Compiled #2 5000   30.00  150.00  750.00   945.00             59  5000.00  1.00
14  Compiled #3 5000   30.00  150.00  750.00   945.00             59  5000.00  1.00
15  Respondent # 5000  75.00  375.00  750.00   945.00             59  5000.00  1.00
16  Respondent # 5000  75.00  375.00  750.00   945.00             59  5000.00  1.00
17  Respondent # 5000  75.00  375.00  750.00   945.00             59  5000.00  1.00
18  Respondent # 5000  75.00  375.00  750.00   945.00             59  5000.00  1.00
19
20    Totals   40000  390.00 1950.00 6000.00  7560.00 2000.00   471 40000.00  1.00
21  -------------------------------------------------------------------------
22  VARIABLE COSTS (PRODUCT/FULFILLMENT)
23
24                  Per Unit
25  Unit Product     15.55                                      7317.65
26  Unit Fulfillment  5.75                                      2705.88
27  Royalty a 12%    10.20                                      4800.00
28  Other             2.25                                      1058.82
29
30                                   Total Variable Costs  15882.35
31  -------------------------------------------------------------------------
32  CALCULATION OF MARGIN
33
34  Total Unit Sales:                                    471
35  Total Fixed Costs:                                 17510.00
36  Total Var. Costs:                                  15882.35
37  Total Revenue:                                     40000.00
38  Breakeven Units:                                     393
39  % Return:                                           0.98%
40  $ Margin:                                          6607.65
41  -------------------------------------------------------------------------
42  COMMENTS:
43
44
45
49
50
51
52
53
54
55
56
57
58
59
```

SAMPLE #3
BREAK-EVEN FORM —
CHANGE IN NUMBER MAILED AND LIST COST

1	A	B	C	D	E	F	G	H	I	J
2	BREAKEVEN ANALYSIS FORM									
3	Date:									
4	Product:									
5	Retail Price $75.00									
6	....									
7	FIXED COSTS (DIRECT MAIL)									
8				LIST	PRINTING	POSTAGE		PROJ.		%
9	LIST	# MLD	CPM	COST	COST	COST	CREATIVE	SALES	REV.	RETURN
10										
11	House File	5000	0.00	0.00	750.00	945.00	2000.00	67	5000.00	1.00
12	Compiled #1	2000	30.00	60.00	300.00	378.00		27	2000.00	1.00
13	Compiled #2	5000	30.00	150.00	750.00	945.00		67	5000.00	1.00
14	Compiled #3	2000	30.00	60.00	300.00	378.00		27	2000.00	1.00
15	Respondent #	5000	55.00	275.00	750.00	945.00		67	5000.00	1.00
16	Respondent #	5000	55.00	275.00	750.00	945.00		67	5000.00	1.00
17	Respondent #	3000	55.00	165.00	450.00	567.00		40	3000.00	1.00
18	Respondent #	3000	75.00	225.00	450.00	567.00		40	3000.00	1.00
19										
20	Totals	30000	330.00	1210.00	4500.00	5670.00	2000.00	400	30000.00	1.00
21	....									
22	VARIABLE COSTS (PRODUCT/FULFILLMENT)									
23										
24			Per Unit							
25	Unit Product		15.55						6220.00	
26	Unit Fulfillment		5.75						2300.00	
27	Royalty @ 12%		9.00						3600.00	
28	Other		2.25						900.00	
29										
30						Total Variable Costs			13020.00	
31	....									
32	CALCULATION OF MARGIN									
33										
34	Total Unit Sales:								400	
35	Total Fixed Costs:								13380.00	
36	Total Var. Costs:								13020.00	
37	Total Revenue:								30000.00	
38	Breakeven Units:								352	
39	% Return:								1.17%	
40	$ Margin:								3600.00	
41	....									
42	COMMENTS:									
43										
44										
45										
49										
50										
51										
52										
53										
54										
55										
56										
57										
58										
59										

SAMPLE #4
BREAK-EVEN FORM —
CHANGE IN PERCENT RETURN

	A	B	C	D	E	F	G	H	I	J
1										
2	BREAKEVEN ANALYSIS FORM									
3	Date:									
4	Product:									
5	Retail Price $75.00									
6	--									
7	FIXED COSTS (DIRECT MAIL)									
8				LIST	PRINTING	POSTAGE		PROJ.		%
9	LIST	# MLD	CPM	COST	COST	COST	CREATIVE	SALES	REV.	RETURN
10										
11	House File	5000	0.00	0.00	750.00	945.00	2000.00	167	12500.00	2.50
12	Compiled #1	5000	30.00	150.00	750.00	945.00		100	7500.00	1.50
13	Compiled #2	5000	30.00	150.00	750.00	945.00		67	5000.00	1.00
14	Compiled #3	5000	30.00	150.00	750.00	945.00		83	6250.00	1.25
15	Respondent #	5000	75.00	375.00	750.00	945.00		67	5000.00	1.00
16	Respondent #	5000	75.00	375.00	750.00	945.00		67	5000.00	1.00
17	Respondent #	5000	75.00	375.00	750.00	945.00		67	5000.00	1.00
18	Respondent #	5000	75.00	375.00	750.00	945.00		67	5000.00	1.00
19										
20	Totals	40000	390.00	1950.00	6000.00	7560.00	2000.00	683	51250.00	1.28
21	--									
22	VARIABLE COSTS (PRODUCT/FULFILLMENT)									
23										
24			Per Unit							
25	Unit Product		15.55						10625.83	
26	Unit Fulfillment		5.75						3929.17	
27	Royalty a 12%		9.00						6150.00	
28	Other		2.25						1537.50	
29										
30						Total Variable Costs			22242.50	
31	--									
32	CALCULATION OF MARGIN									
33										
34	Total Unit Sales:								683	
35	Total Fixed Costs:								17510.00	
36	Total Var. Costs:								22242.50	
37	Total Revenue:								51250.00	
38	Breakeven Units:								530	
39	% Return:								1.33%	
40	$ Margin:								11497.50	
41	--									
42	COMMENTS:									
43										
44										
45										
49										
50										
51										
52										
53										
54										
55										
56										
57										
58										
59										

SAMPLE #5
BREAK-EVEN FORM —
CHANGE IN VARIABLE COSTS

1	A	B	C	D	E	F	G	H	I	J
2	BREAKEVEN ANALYSIS FORM									
3	Date:									
4	Product:									
5	Retail Price	$75.00								
6	-------									
7	FIXED COSTS (DIRECT MAIL)									
8				LIST	PRINTING	POSTAGE		PROJ.		%
9	LIST	# MLD	CPM	COST	COST	COST	CREATIVE	SALES	REV.	RETURN
10										
11	House File	5000	0.00	0.00	750.00	945.00	2000.00	67	5000.00	1.00
12	Compiled #1	5000	30.00	150.00	750.00	945.00		67	5000.00	1.00
13	Compiled #2	5000	30.00	150.00	750.00	945.00		67	5000.00	1.00
14	Compiled #3	5000	30.00	150.00	750.00	945.00		67	5000.00	1.00
15	Respondent #	5000	75.00	375.00	750.00	945.00		67	5000.00	1.00
16	Respondent #	5000	75.00	375.00	750.00	945.00		67	5000.00	1.00
17	Respondent #	5000	75.00	375.00	750.00	945.00		67	5000.00	1.00
18	Respondent #	5000	75.00	375.00	750.00	945.00		67	5000.00	1.00
19										
20	Totals	40000	390.00	1950.00	6000.00	7560.00	2000.00	533	40000.00	1.00
21	-------									
22	VARIABLE COSTS (PRODUCT/FULFILLMENT)									
23										
24			Per Unit							
25	Unit Product		12.75						6800.00	
26	Unit Fulfillment		3.75						2000.00	
27	Royalty @ 10%		7.50						4000.00	
28	Other		2.25						1200.00	
29										
30							Total Variable Costs		14000.00	
31	-------									
32	CALCULATION OF MARGIN									
33										
34	Total Unit Sales:								533	
35	Total Fixed Costs:								17510.00	
36	Total Var. Costs:								14000.00	
37	Total Revenue:								40000.00	
38	Breakeven Units:								420	
39	% Return:								1.05%	
40	$ Margin:								8490.00	
41	-------									
42	COMMENTS:									
43										
44										
45										
49										
50										
51										
52										
53										
54										
55										
56										
57										
58										
59										

SAMPLE #6
FORMULAS FOR BREAK-EVEN SPREADSHEET

	A	B	C	D	E	F	G	H	I	J
1										
2										
3										
4	BREAKEVEN ANALYSIS FORM									
5										
6	Date:									
7	Product:									
8	Retail Price	$400.00								
9										
10	FIXED COSTS (DIRECT MAIL)									
11										
12	LIST	# MLD	CPM	LIST COST	PRINTING COST	POSTAGE COST	CREATIVE	PROJ. SALES	REV.	% RETURN
13										
14	House File	0	0.00	+B14/1000*C14	+$1400.00	+$1400.18%	0.00	+14/C8	+$14*J14	+AVG(J14..J21)
15	Compiled #1	0	0.00	+B15/1000*C15	+$1340.00	+$1340.18%		+15/C9	+$15*J15	
16	Compiled #2	0	0.00	+B16/1000*C16	+$1340.00	+$1340.18%		+16/C10	+$16*J16	
17	Compiled #3	0	0.00	+B17/1000*C17	+$1740.00	+$1740.18%		+17/C11	+$17*J17	
18	Respondent #	0	0.00	+B18/1000*C18	+$1840.00	+$1840.18%		+18/C12	+$18*J18	
19	Respondent #	0	0.00	+B19/1000*C19	+$1940.00	+$1940.18%		+19/C13	+$19*J19	
20	Respondent #	0	0.00	+B20/1000*C20	+$2040.00	+$2040.18%		+20/C14	+$204*J20	
21	Respondent #	0	0.00	+B21/1000*C21	+$2140.00	+$2140.18%		+21/C15	+$214*J21	
22										
23	Totals	@SUM(B14..B21)	@SUM(C14..C21)	@SUM(D14..D21)	@SUM(E14..E21)	@SUM(F14..F21)	@SUM(G14..G21)	@SUM(H14..H21)	@AVG(J14..J21)	
24	VARIABLE COSTS (PRODUCT/FULFILLMENT)									
25										
26										
27			Per Unit							
28	Unit Product		0.00							
29	Unit Fulfillment		0.00							
30	Royalty @ 12%		+$840.00							
31	Other		0.00							
32										
33						Total Variable Costs			@SUM(I28..I31)	
34										
35	CALCULATION OF MARGIN									
36										
37	Total Unit Sales:								+H23	
38	Total Fixed Costs:								@SUM(D20..G20)	
39	Total Var. Costs:								+I33	
40	Total Revenue:								+I23	
41	Breakeven Units:								(I38+I39)/I40	
42	% Return:								+I41/I23	
43	% Margin:								+H40-(H38+H39)	
44										
45	COMMENTS:									
46										
47										
48										
49										
50										

2. Write your advertising for the right people

You need to create your advertising for those people who are your best prospects. In direct mail, you want to talk only to potential customers, not to anyone who might have a mild interest in your product. Learn to target your sales message.

3. Don't worry about whether people will "like" your advertising

You don't need to win awards to have good advertising. You don't even need to make your friends happy with what you're doing. All you're really looking for is response. You need only be concerned with whether your advertising is informative and persuasive enough to get action.

4. Don't be obsessed with the competition to the detriment of your sales message

Don't spend so much time fighting your competition, comparing your products and services to theirs, etc., that you don't tell the reader how he or she can benefit from your product.

5. Hit them with your best shot first

You can't save the best for last in direct mail. You have to hit your prospects with your strongest sales argument first. If you start off weak, you may lose your reader, and you won't get a second chance.

6. Don't talk features instead of benefits

Don't tell a customer about the product specifications and quality materials your product has to offer. Do tell the customer what these features mean to him or her.

7. Establish a need for what you're selling

If you don't establish the need for your product, you can't possibly convince someone to make the purchasing decision. If the customer doesn't recognize a problem, why would he or she buy your solution for that problem?

8. Don't say it if you can't prove it

Any advertiser can make claims. These claims will only be believed, though, if they are backed up with proof. Use testimonials and case histories whenever possible. Try to support every claim you make.

h. COMMON DIRECT MAIL BLUNDERS AND HOW TO AVOID THEM

So far in this chapter we have taken a broad view of the elements needed for a successful direct mail campaign. Now let's look at some of the elements that can hamper (or even ruin) those campaigns.

1. Choosing the wrong mailing list

In direct mail there is nothing more important than the list you use. The list you choose will depend on the product you're marketing and your decision should be based on the characteristics of the people whose names make up the list. For example, suppose you're introducing a new needlepoint kit and you're deliberating between five lists:

(a) People who are hobbyists

(b) People who belong to a needlepoint association

(c) People who have purchased needlepoint kits from a competitor

(d) People who shop at a jewelry boutique in the same block as your store

(e) Your own customers who have previously purchased needlepoint kits

The best list will always be your own customers who have purchased or shown an interest in similar products. The next best list would be people who had purchased a similar product from another company. Known purchasers of like products are always the best source when searching for a mailing list. But, if those types of lists aren't available, the next

30

best choice would be a list comprised of people who show an affinity for your product.

For instance, a group of people in a needlepoint association would probably be interested in purchasing a needlepoint kit and, on a broader scale, so might a group of people who are known hobbyists.

The customer list from the nearby jewelry boutique would be the poorest choice. The people on that list may shop and live near your store, but only a tiny percentage of them would be needlepoint fans and, therefore, likely to be interested in what you are selling. When choosing a list, you want to find the most highly segmented group possible to keep your mailing numbers (and therefore your expenses) as low as possible. The key, therefore, is to use a rifle rather than a shotgun approach to reaching potential customers.

Chapters 4 and 5 discuss mailing lists in detail.

2. Not having a clear concept of your offer

What are you selling?

This may seem like a very simple question, but sometimes it's more complicated than it appears. Your offer needs to be as simple and compelling as possible. That means that if you're trying to sell more than one thing at a time you need to either highlight one of the items or package the items together in a natural grouping. Offering too many choices can confuse your customers and result in a negative response to all items.

Another aspect of the offer is how it is structured. Consider the following offers:

- Buy one — get one free

- Buy one and get ½ off

- Buy one — get the second for 1¢

31

They all mean essentially the same thing, but the response to each could be different. You'll want to test the impact of various offers on your market.

You also need to consider carefully the terms of sale:

- cash up front,

- bill later,

- 30-day free trial, and

- full guarantee,

are all terms that can influence the purchase decision of your market. A guarantee is especially important in direct mail. Ordering through direct mail involves some potential risk to the customer. What if they don't like the product? What if it doesn't live up to their expectations? A generous return policy serves as a potent "risk reliever" that can boost sales.

Many direct marketers spend far too little time on developing a clear offer. Don't make this mistake. Be sure that you know what you're selling and on what terms you're selling it. Then present the offer clearly and simply. We'll be taking a more detailed look at developing a direct mail offer in chapter 9.

3. Trying to be all things to all people

If your target market is too broad and too varied, it's impossible to develop a marketing approach that will be specific enough to that market's needs to reap the response you want. Your product may, indeed, appeal to many different types of people. But, if this is the case, it's important that you take the time to develop different mailings for each of these groups so that your copy can be personalized to their individual needs.

For instance, let's return to the needlepoint kit example. When you're mailing to purchasers of your own products, your letter could take this tone:

> "You recently purchased X-kit from us. Now we've come out with a brand new kit that we think you'll like even better. Like the kit you already own, it comes with easy-to-understand instructions. But, this new kit..."

When promoting the kit to members of a hobbyist group, on the other hand, your approach should be different:

> "You're a hobbyist. You enjoy the personal satisfaction of creating something on your own — something beautiful and lasting. That's why we feel you'll appreciate our new XYZ needlepoint kit. If you're never tried needlepoint, you'll find that it's... If you're already an old pro, you'll ..."

Gear your copy to your audience and try to deal with the most narrow market segments you can find. The more specific your appeal is to your audience, the more closely you can tie the benefits of your product to their individual needs. And, speaking of copy...

4. Not paying enough attention to copy

You've got a sure-fire product, an irresistible offer and a very specific, clearly identified market. The rest is simple, right?

Wrong.

Many marketers feel that once they've found or developed a great product and identified an appropriate list, everything else simply falls into place. They fail to appreciate the importance of developing strong promotional copy.

Don't throw together a quick letter at the last minute after you've spent hours on every other aspect of your campaign. When developing copy, make sure that you do the following:

(a)   Tell enough

Study after study, test after test, shows that long copy outpulls short copy. As the old maxim goes, "the more you tell, the more you sell." Don't skimp on copy — write enough to fully describe your product and how it will benefit your potential audience, but...

(b) Know when to stop

You can go too far in writing about your product. The key is to focus on one major benefit and to provide the customer with as much pertinent information as is necessary for them to make a buying decision.

(c) Focus on benefits

Don't tell how proud you are of your product and how expertly it's crafted. Translate those features into benefits for your audience. Instead of saying, "our detailed instructions include step-by-step guidelines that have been developed after hours of careful deliberation..." say, "you'll save time and avoid frustration with the easy-to-follow instructions included with our XYZ kit."

(d) Anticipate and respond to every possible objection

Your copy is really your salesperson and, in direct mail, your only chance to close the sale. With a direct mail letter or brochure you don't get the opportunity to explain what you meant if it's unclear. You don't get the chance to answer unanswered questions. Don't be vague, thinking that readers will understand what you mean. Say what you mean clearly and succinctly. Ask several people to read your copy to make sure that you haven't left anything out and that you've answered the questions they have about your product and your offer. We'll take a more detailed look at copy development in chapter 6.

5. Failing to test (and retest)

You've found a list and developed a direct mail letter that yields a response beyond your wildest expectations. Don't make the mistake of feeling that your job is done and that you can just sit back and continue to mail the same letter to the same group of people over and over again.

Perhaps another letter in a different format or with a different offer would work better. Perhaps another list will yield an even greater response. You'll never know unless you test.

Most direct marketers test continually against a proven "control." When another effort, after a series of tests, proves to be a more effective mailing, it becomes the new control — and so on. Never become complacent as a direct marketer. The direct mail industry is a volatile one — what works one month may not work well the next. We'll take a more detailed look at testing in chapter 10.

6. Overlooking the importance of the response vehicle

Make it easy to order. The order form is often the most overlooked aspect of the direct mail piece. It's thrown together in a hurry and often fails to —

(a) Remind the prospect of why he or she should order,

(b) Restate the offer clearly,

(c) Provide precise instructions on how to order (you'd be amazed at how many people forget to include a return address!), and

(d) Ask for all the necessary information.

For more on order forms, see chapter 9.

7. Not knowing when to quit

Your new product has been getting a great response and you've been mailing like crazy. Don't be too "mail-happy." Keep a close eye on response or you'll find yourself throwing back all the money you make on your initial efforts.

Unless you're faced with a continuously growing market or an insatiable need, there will come a point when your promotions begin to lose their effectiveness. If you're not monitoring your response closely, you may very well miss that point and continue to promote. The result? You're spending all the money you made originally in a feeble attempt to gain new sales.

If your product has reached the point of market saturation and you're beginning to throw away the money you've made, it's time to "backlist" that item and cut back on promotions. Continue to promote, but consider less expensive efforts like ridealong announcements with other orders or a listing in your product catalog.

i. CONCLUSION

Direct mail is a deceptively simple form of advertising. Simple — because just about anybody can choose a list, write a letter and do a mailing. Deceptive — because it's not as easy as it looks. Be cautious as you embark on a direct mail program: do your behind-the-scenes work, recognize the elements of a successful campaign, and avoid the potential blunders that many mailers fall prey to.

3

POSTAL REGULATIONS

"Mail" is the operative word in the term "direct mail marketing." Without a good understanding of how to use the postal system effectively, a direct mailer has virtually no chance of succeeding.

a. THIRD-CLASS MAIL OR ADMAIL

Let's first discuss the type of mail service you will most likely use: third-class mail, in the United States, or Admail, in Canada.

1. U.S. third-class mail

The U.S. Postal Service defines third-class mail as "printed matter weighing less than 16 ounces." Printed matter means material that consists of words, letters, characters, figures, or images, or any combination of them not having the character of a bill or statement of account, or of actual or personal correspondence, which has been reproduced by any other process than handwriting or typewriting.

The U.S. post office outlines the main points of bulk mailings as follows:

(a) There must be a minimum of at least 200 pieces or 50 pounds for each mailing and the pieces must be identical in size, weight, and enclosures, if the permit imprint is used.

(b) Postage payment for each mailing must be prepaid by one of three methods: postage meter, precancelled stamps, or permit imprint.

(c) Each piece must have a ZIP Code and the mail must be sorted into packages by ZIP code. Sack minimums are 125 pieces or 15 pounds per sack. (Sorting will be discussed in more detail later.)

(d) A properly completed mailing statement must accompany each mailing presented.

(e) Each piece must have a destination city name. The word "CITY" is not acceptable.

A mailing cannot be accepted as bulk mail if it contains —

(a) hand or typewritten personalized messages (with the exception of signature),

(b) bills or statements of any kind, or

(c) any matter which does not specifically identify the permit holder as the mailer.

2. Canadian Admail

Canada Post requires that items posted at the Admail (or Bulk Third Class) rate of postage must be printed matter, advertising, etc., and not defined as first class mail, and that the items must be identical, as follows:

(a) same size and shape,

(b) same return address and/or company name, and

(c) all weighing under 50 grams or all weighing over 50 grams.

Other Admail regulations include the following:

(a) The minimum quantity per single mailing is 5,000 provincially or 10,000 nationally. Smaller quantities may be mailed provided that a permit number is used and that the required minimum quantity is paid for.

(b) Items weighing over 50 grams must be mailed under permit.

(c) All addresses must include postal codes.

(d) Mail must be sorted according to the National Distribution Guide.

(e) If metered, items must include a "BULK" endorsement next to the meter impression.

(f) Mail must be deposited in a postal plant with a Postage-Paid-In-Cash (PPIC) statement.

(g) Mailings of more than 25,000 items must be scheduled for deposit into a plant.

b. GETTING HELP

One of the most important considerations to keep in mind when working with either the U.S. or the Canadian post office is that they are eager to work with you and to help you meet their requirements and specifications. Their goal is to process the mail — all mail — as efficiently as possible. By working with you to ensure your compliance with the requirements, they are able to meet that goal more effectively.

As a result, postal authorities are glad to explain the procedures to you and to keep you informed of new regulations and new ways that you can operate more effectively — including ways to save money.

While the tomes of material provided by the postal system may, upon first glance, seem intimidating, the system can be simplified into four areas:

(a) Postage

(b) Format

(c) Sorting

(d) Rates

c. POSTAGE

1. Postage meters

A postage meter is obtained from a postage meter company and postage is then affixed by meter print or meter tape. Postage is deducted each time a piece is placed through the meter. The post office recommends that, when using a postage meter, the date be omitted from the mailing piece itself. Month and year is sufficient. Why? Because, if you place a specific date on your mail, it must be the actual date of mailing. Leaving the date off is to your advantage since delays could cause you to have to re-meter your mail and, in the process, you could lose hundreds (even thousands) of outer envelopes that are no longer usable.

In the U.S., you can receive a partial reimbursement for spoiled or unused envelopes and meter tapes by bringing them to the post office within one year of the date. The post office will give you a 90 percent rebate for the postage on unused pieces.

In Canada, you can obtain a 90 percent refund for unused metered mail by bringing the unused envelopes to the post office. For unused meter tapes, the post office will either issue a refund or adjust the reading on your meter, depending on the type of meter you have.

Many direct mailers find that metered postage is quite effective when used with a window envelope because it gives the mailing the look of an invoice, which means that a high percentage of your mailing pieces will get opened. However, keep in mind that the reverse is also true: when used on non-window, labeled envelopes, metered postage often gets low readership because of its junk-mail look.

2. Precanceled stamps

In the U.S., precanceled stamps can be purchased at the post office and are available only in rolls of 500. These stamps are affixed just as any stamp is. The post office recommends that you contact them two or three days before your mailing date to make sure that the quantity you need is available.

Stamps can be used for any class of postage, but they create the impression of first-class, personal mail. While it can cost between $5 and $12 per thousand to hand-affix stamps in a large volume, many mailers have found that this "personal" touch increases response.

Precancelled stamps are not available in Canada.

3. Permits

A permit imprint is a printed or rubber-stamped impression of a rectangular box containing information about class of mail, location of mailer, and mailer's permit number. Postage is charged by counting pieces and deducting the total postage from a fund which is opened in the permit holder's name. This method allows you to mail without handling each piece and is the most popular way of affixing postage.

In the U.S., there is a one-time charge of $75.* You must do at least one mailing using your permit imprint during the 12 months after the date of purchase. The permit imprint privilege then remains valid for the 12 months following each of your last mailings. If you do not mail within a 12-month period, the imprint becomes invalid.

At the time you request a permit number, a trust fund will be established in your name. Before doing a mailing, you must deposit an amount sufficient to cover the cost of postage for that mailing. No mail will be accepted if funds are not sufficient to cover the cost of postage.

You can obtain a permit number by going to a post office and paying the fee. The permit number is used to stamp (or pre-print) each piece of mail in the upper right-hand corner

---

*Fees given are accurate at time of publication but are subject to change without notice. Be sure to confirm all fees with the appropriate office before submitting any fees.

of the mailing area. On an envelope, this is the upper right-hand corner of the envelope itself.

In Canada, there is no charge for a bulk rate mailing permit. To receive a permit number, simply call Canada Post and request one. The permit does not expire; you would only need a new number if regulations were to change — e.g., when barcodes come into use.

d. FORMAT

The format of your mailings must conform to standard postal requirements in order to be mailed.

In the United States, bulk mail is divided into three categories:

(a) Letter-size mail

(b) Non-letter or flat-size mail

(c) Machinable parcels

Letter-size mail must be:

- minimum $3\frac{1}{2}$" x 5"
- maximum $6\frac{1}{2}$" x $11\frac{1}{2}$"
- minimum thickness .007"
- maximum thickness $\frac{1}{2}$".

Non-letter or flat-size mail consists of unwrapped, paper-wrapped, sleeve-wrapped, and enveloped matter that exceeds one or more of the dimensions of letter-size mail, but does not exceed the dimensions of:

- $6\frac{1}{8}$" high x $11\frac{1}{2}$" long x $\frac{1}{2}$" thick.

Machinable parcels must be:

- minimum of 3" x 6", $\frac{1}{2}$" thick, 8 oz., and
- maximum of 17" x 34", 17" thick, and 35 lbs. in weight.

You should try to take advantage of the opportunities presented by conforming your mailings to machinable requirements. The requirements for automatable mail take into account physical characteristics of the piece, readability, address accuracy, and format. The post office is concerned with these characteristics because optical character readers (OCRs) have problems with mail that is too floppy, too rigid, too big or too small, weighs too much, isn't readily readable, has addresses located in odd places, etc. The requirements for automatable mail are as follows:

(a) Pieces must be 5" wide x 3½" high, minimum, to 11½" wide x 6⅛" high, maximum.

(b) Minimum thickness for the smaller pieces is .007", for the larger pieces .009." Maximum thickness is .025."

(c) And (here's where you'll have to draw upon your mathematics skills), all pieces must be rectangular and the aspect ratio (length divided by height) must fall between 1.3 and 2.5. To qualify for automation discounts, avoid mailers of extreme length or with odd shapes.

(d) The entire address must be located in a defined "OCR read area" (see Sample #7). Before February 1992, this area is 1" from either side; after February 1992, it is ½". Further, the top line of the address block must be 2¾" from the bottom of the piece and the bottom line must be ⅝" from the bottom.

(e) Placing a return address in the OCR read area is prohibited.

(f) Mail must be in a sealed envelope or be sealed on all four edges (except for self-mailers, double postcards, and booklet-type mailing pieces).

(g) The folded edge of self-mailers, double postcards, and booklets must be the bottom edge of the mail piece in relation to the address. Two tabs must be

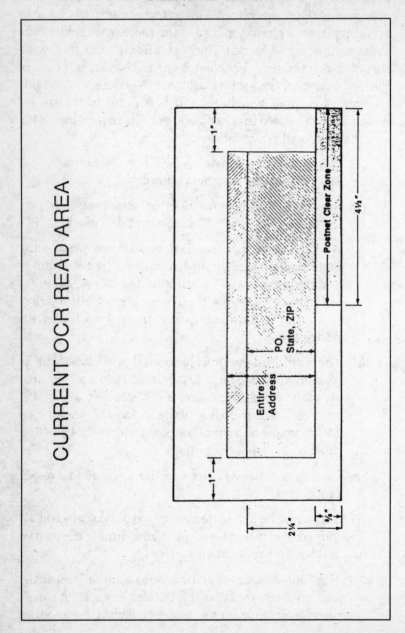

CURRENT OCR READ AREA

Sealing - Folding - Tabbing
Before February 2, 1992

Minimum Requirements

BOOKLET

Tabs - 2 (1 inch from edge)
Fold/Spine - Bottom Only
Sheets - Multiple with cover
20 lbs. basis weight

DOUBLE POSTCARD

Tabs - 1 (Middle of Piece)
Fold - top or bottom
Sheets - Single
75 lbs. basis weight

FOLDED SELF-MAILER

Tabs - 1 (Middle of Piece)
Fold - top or bottom
Sheets - Multiple or single
20 lbs. basis weight

Tab, Wafer Seal, or Spot Clue

Sealing - Folding - Tabbing
After February 2, 1992

FOLDED SELF-MAILER

Tabs - 2 (1 inch from edge)
Fold - top or bottom
Sheets - Multiple or single
20 lbs. basis weight

FOLDED SELF-MAILER

Tabs - 1 (Middle of piece)
Fold - Bottom
Sheets - Multiple
24 lbs. basis weight

FOLDED SELF-MAILER

Tabs - 1 (Middle of piece)
Fold - Bottom
Sheets - Single
28 lbs. basis weight

Tab, Wafer Seal, or Spot Clue

placed on the top edge of each piece within one inch each of the upper left and upper right edges on the piece. The top edge can be spot glued or continuously glued (see Sample #8).

(h) Poly-wrapped or poly-bagged pieces will not qualify for automation-based rates, nor will mailing pieces that contain rigid items (such as pens, pencils, keys, etc.). Small coins and tokens may be included if they are firmly affixed to part of the contents.

For further information on these requirements, ask your postmaster for a copy of USPS Publication #67, *Automation Plan for Business Mailers*, and USPS Publication #25, *A Guide to Business Mail Preparation*.

If you are dealing with U.S. postal regulations, another resource that should never be far from your side is *The Domestic Mail Manual*, the bible of the direct mail industry when it comes to postal guidelines. It's available from the Government Printing Office, Washington, D.C. 20402-9371 (or phone 202-783-3238) and costs $19 a year.

The postal service is happy to advise mailers and encourages (but does not require) mailers to submit designs *before printing* to ensure compliance.

In Canada, the following size and weight standards must be adhered to:

- maximum size, 38 cm (length) x 27 cm (width) x 2 cm (thickness),

- minimum size, 10 cm (length) x 7 cm (width) x 0.18 cm (thickness),

- maximum weight, 500 grams.

Small items such as pens and keys may be included if they are packaged securely enough that they will not break out of the envelope.

Canada Post's commercial service reps are available to look over your mailing items for you, to ensure that they meet Admail requirements.

e. SORTING

The most important step in preparing mail is sorting, which includes labeling, packaging, and sacking.

In the United States, the post office will supply mailers with the materials they need to properly prepare mail (e.g., trays, rubber bands, and label stickers), at no cost.

In Canada, the post office supplies mailbags only.

If you do not have a labeling machine and do not use an outside mailing service, you should request your labels in sticky-label format so that they can be hand-affixed. With large numbers, however, this process becomes unwieldy; you would be well advised either to use the services available from letter shops or to buy your own equipment.

Once your mailing pieces have been prepared and labeled, the next step is to sort and label them. All mail must be sorted by zip code or postal code. It is thus extremely important, when ordering your mailing lists, to ask that they be sent to you in zip code order. Imagine the problem you'd be faced with if you received 10,000 labels in random order and had to sort them yourself!

1. U.S. sorting requirements

In order to qualify for the lowest possible rates, mail must be sorted as specifically as possible, into direct sacks, 3-digit sacks, and state sacks.

(a) Direct

The direct sack is for mail that is all going to the same zip code. There must be a minimum of 125 pieces or 15 pounds of mail for the same 5-digit zip area. Each individual package should not exceed 4". The post office prefers that you secure these packages with rubber bands.

(b) 3-digit

The 3-digit sack is for mail that is all going to the same SCF (first three digits of the zip code). There must be a minimum of 125 pieces or 15 pounds of mail for the same 3-digit zip area. The first three digits must be the same for all pieces; the last two may vary.

(c) State

The state sack is for mail that is all going to the same state. There must be a minimum of ten pieces.

(d) Miscellaneous

The miscellaneous bag is for all remaining mail — that which could not be placed in any of the previous three sacks.

2. Canadian sorting requirements

Mail must be sorted, bundled, and bagged according to the National Distribution Guide, available at post offices. The three categories are:

- NDG mixed,
- direct bundles, and
- letter carrier presort.

In NDG mixed, all mail in one bag goes to one postal outlet. Direct bundles contain items that are all going to the same first three digits of the postal code. Letter carrier presort requires items to be sorted by walk; it is usually done only with mailings of over 5,000 provincially or 10,000 nationally.

f. RATES

Postal rates and requirements change frequently. In order to be sure you have the most current information, you must check with the post office.

In the United States, using barcodes on outgoing mail can provide further discounts. Barcoding is a computerized coding system that allows mail to go through the mail stream faster: optical readers scan the code and interpret the address based on that code.

In both the United States and Canada, a bar code representing your own address can be used in business reply mail.

4

RENTING MAILING LISTS

The mailing list is the most important element of a successful direct mail program. The list is your market and it is the aspect of this form of marketing that makes it so special and so specialized. You have two options for obtaining lists for your marketing efforts —

(a) rent a list from someone else, or

(b) build your own list.

This chapter discusses the first option, while chapter 5 deals with building your own list.

a. WHAT ARE MAILING LISTS?

To those who are newly introduced to direct mail, the concept of mailing lists can be a heady discovery. A mailing list is simply a list of names and addresses of businesses or individuals. This basic information can be enhanced with other bits of data that are added to the record. For instance, one label on a list you purchase might look like this:

Joe Blow
1782 N. Highland Ave.
Chicago, IL 60410

Within the computer where that name was stored, there might exist a lot of other details about Joe. If this name was provided by a company that Joe did business with, they have a list of the items he has purchased, the dates he purchased them, and how much he paid. They probably also have his telephone number. They may also have his age, his occupation, his household income, and any number of other details about Joe.

Computers have made it possible to gather and maintain amazing amounts of data on individuals. One database can now be combined (or enhanced) with data from another database to create a single database that is filled with information about a particular prospect. All of this information allows you to be very particular when you're placing a list order. It helps you target your market so you don't waste your advertising dollars sending mail to people who are very unlikely to be interested. You can be assured that you're getting information about your product to the people who are most likely to purchase. There are two major types of lists: compiled and respondent. These will be discussed later in this chapter in sections **e.** and **f.**

When you pay someone else to use their mailing list, keep in mind that you are renting and not purchasing that list. And you are renting it for one-time use only unless you have made other arrangements. Lists are considered valuable commodities by their owners and infringement of their use is considered a theft just like any other theft. Take precautions so that you do not inadvertently or otherwise use a list or any portion of it more than once.

How much can you expect to pay for a list? Compiled lists usually rent in the $30-45/m area, while respondent lists can be priced as high as $150/m. (/m means *per thousand*.) That's just the base price. The actual cost will depend on whether you choose various selects (options) or include key codes on the list. See section **c.** below for further discussion of these topics.

b. HOW ARE MAILING LISTS BUILT?

A name may exist on many different lists. That's why you get all that mail that some people refer to disparagingly as "junk mail." How did all those companies get your name? In any number of ways. In fact, it's virtually impossible to get your name removed from all lists. The closest you can come is contacting the Direct Marketing Association to ask that your name be placed on their Mail Preference Service list. This is a service whereby consumers who do not wish to receive mail advertising can request that their names be removed from large numbers of mailing lists. Companies are not required to participate in this service, however, so even taking this step will not assure that you will no longer receive any unsolicited mail.

Consider how your name gets on these lists in the first place. Do you have a listed telephone number? Many companies compile their lists directly from telephone directories. Are you registered to vote? Have you ever bought a car? Rented or bought a home? Subscribed to a magazine? Or, the most obvious, purchased something through the mail?

Once you do any of these things, your name is on the market. And, once on the market, it's quickly bandied about until your name can be on countless databases ready to be rented by a mailer.

If you're curious about watching how your name is rented, you can do this: reply to a direct mail solicitation using a slight variation of your name. Then watch the mailing labels on your mail to see which are carrying that variation. For instance, if I send for an Avon clothing catalog using the name Linda Richards (my maiden name), within two to three months I'll probably receive a catalog from The Ultimate, Spiegel's, and even Frederick's of Hollywood! It's an interesting exercise and one that helps you become familiar with the fast-paced nature of the mailing industry.

c. THE PLAYERS IN THE LIST INDUSTRY

1. List Brokers

Where do you get lists? From list brokers. Yes, lists are such big business that there are hundreds of people who have set up companies for the sole purpose of renting these lists. Why? Because there are millions of names that can be listed in an infinite variety of ways. While you can attempt to research the list market yourself and order directly from the list source, (a magazine publisher, for example), it's much simpler to use a list broker. The list broker will coordinate all the necessary arrangements for ordering your lists, help you with list research, and make recommendations to you on list selections. And the broker can provide you with countless tips and inside information that you would not have been able to find on your own. All at no charge to you!

List brokers make their money by charging a commission to the person renting the list. A magazine publisher, for example, might charge $80/m (/m = per thousand) for a list. The broker would get 15 % or $12 for every thousand names. Considering that many large companies mail many millions of names each year, you can easily see why renting lists can get to be big business.

2.   List managers

List managers promote and rent lists for someone else. List managers act as the exclusive market or source for information on certain lists. List brokers may also play the role of list manager and some lists are managed in-house. For instance, a magazine publisher may manage its own list rather than using an outside source.

3.   List compiliers

List compilers are people who develop lists of names and addresses. These names and addresses are drawn from many sources, including directories, public records, and membership rosters.

4.   Rate Cards

Another source of information about list availability is the rate or data card. This card presents much the same information as you'll find in the SRDS. Once your company is identified as a

1990

Registered Nurses

2,177,140   Registered nurse prospects $40/M

Also available:

413,134	RN magazine subscribers .... (see separate card)	$65/M
101,640	RN magazine expires .... (see separate card)	$40/M
39,378	Nurse bookbuyers .... (see separate card)	$65/M
43,623	Nurse PDR® buyers .... (see separate card)	$65/M

Registered nurse prospects are names gathered from state registers. This compiled list is updated quarterly from current source lists and NCOA corrected.

Primarily working women; frequently bringing in a second income. This list is perfect for business and consumer offers. It may also be used for recruitment.

LPNs also available .... Please inquire.

Contact Mary Bousfield or Barbara Brennan at 201-262-3030 or 800-223-0581.
Fax number is 201-262-5461 and 201-262-2760.

Orders cancelled after mail date require payment in full.

Selections
5 digit Zip $5/M
3 digit SCF $5/M
State $3/M
Nth $3/M

Minimum Order $250

Output
4 up cheshire .... Std., n/c
9/1600 BPI tape $25
Pressure labels $7.50/M
Keying $1/M
Splits (each) $50

Updated: Quarterly

©1990 Medical Economics Company, Inc.
all rights reserved.

MEDEC LIST MARKETING

MEDICAL ECONOMICS COMPANY
Oradell, New Jersey 07649-9986

Patricia McKeon
List Manager
201 262-3030
800 223-0581

1

potential mailer, you'll receive these cards on a regular basis through the mail (yes, your name is now on these people's lists!) as new lists become available (see Sample #9).

d. WORKING WITH A BROKER

If you're using a broker, make sure he or she really understands your business. Many brokers are specialists whose knowledge of your particular business may be minimal if your business is not the one the broker specializes in. If that's the case, you may find that the information you're getting from your broker is no more detailed than what you could find yourself.

Your broker should be like a partner in your operation. The broker needs to know what you're selling, who your market is, what your promotional mailings are like, and, ultimately, how well each of your mailings is working. If you don't provide this information, you won't be getting the quality of service that can help boost your responses.

You shouldn't have to be a large mailer to get quality attention from list brokers. A good broker will realize that your business has potential for growth in the future (we'll assume that it does) and will want to work with you now even though your orders may be small. Why? Because that broker is hoping that, as your needs grow, you'll continue to rely on the same service you got when you were starting out.

e. COMPILED LISTS

A compiled list is a list of people who share a common characteristic. For instance, they may all be members of a certain association or a certain profession — a list of attorneys, for example. Or a list of new mothers. But that's all they are. They are not necessarily direct mail purchasers. All you know about them is that they share a certain characteristic.

1. Standard Industrial Classification Codes (SIC)

Compiled lists are used most often by business-to-business mailers who select these lists based on Standard Industrial Classification (SIC) codes.

SIC codes are four digit codes under which different types of businesses are classified. In some cases, a 4 + 4 digit code is used which provides greater selectivity. The codes start at 0100 for agriculture and go through 9900 for non-classifiable establishments. Within this range are listings for companies as diverse and specialized as Jewish synagogues, taxidermists, and carnival supply wholesalers (see Sample #10).

All major list companies publish their own catalog of SIC codes, but these codes are standard and don't vary from one company to another. In fact, there are only three major list compilers; the other brokers get their compiled lists directly from these compilers.

When you order by SIC you get a list of business names and addresses — not necessarily of individuals within those businesses. Make sure that you ask whether or not the labels are addressed to individuals. If not, and you want to target a specific position, you can do so by adding "title slugs," which are generated by the computer at the time the labels are printed. For instance, you might do a mailing to banks (SIC 6020) and add the title slug "loan officer" if you thought that person would be most likely to respond to your offer.

While compiled files do not represent "known buyers," these lists are becoming increasingly sophisticated through the addition of various selection options related to both demographics and psychographics. This information is collected by compilers and used to enhance files, thus offering direct marketers a wider variety of options when using compiled files.

3662 – 4521

SIC NO.	DESCRIPTION	QUANTITY
3662	Radio & TV communication equipment mfrs.	4,086
3670	Electronic components & accessories manufacturers (SIC 3670-3679)	7,202
3674	Semiconductor & related devices manufacturers	1,791
3677	Electronic coil & transformers mfrs.	541
3678	Electronic connector mfrs.	192
3679	Electronic components manufacturers, misc.	5,297
3690	Storage battery & other misc. equipment mfrs. (SIC 3690-3699)	1,255
3691	Battery, storage	278
3692	Battery, primary & wet	118
3693	X-ray apparatus & tube manufacturers	425
3694	Engine elec. equip. mfrs.	686
3699	Elec. equipment mfrs.	736
3700	Transportation equipment manufacturers (SIC 3700-3799)	19,210
3711	Motor vehicle mfrs.	891
3713	Truck & bus body mfrs.	1,166
3714	Motor vehicle parts & accessories mfrs.	3,831
3715	Truck trailer mfrs.	644
3721	Aircraft manufacturers	240
3724	Aircraft engines & parts	422
3728	Aircraft equipment, misc.	818
3731	Ship building & repairing yards	805
3732	Boat building & repairing	7,630
3732A	Boat repair yards	5,275
3732B	Boat building & repairing yards	2,097
3743	Railroad equipment mfrs.	342
3751	Motorcycle & bicycle parts manufacturers	378
3760	Space vehicle, guided missile & equip. mfrs.	251
3792	Travel trailer & camper manufacturers	755
3799	Transportation equipment manufacturers, misc.	611
3800	Measuring, analyzing & controlling instruments; photographic, medical & optical goods; watch & clock manufacturers (SIC 3800-3873)	13,961
3811	Engineering & scientific instruments mfrs.	1,629
3822	Environ. controls mfrs.	756
3823	Measurement & control devices manufacturers	2,085
3824	Fluid meters & counting devices manufacturers	407
3825	Electricity measuring devices manufacturers	1,347
3829	Measuring & control devices manufacturers, misc.	1,106
3832	Optical instrument & lens manufacturers	831
3841	Surgical & medical instruments mfrs.	1,367
3842	Surgical supplies & appliances mfrs.	1,882
3843	Dental equipment & supplies manufacturers	778

SIC NO.	DESCRIPTION	QUANTITY
3851	Ophthalmic goods mfrs.	1,080
3861	Photographic equipment & supplies mfrs.	1,252
3873	Watch, clock & clockworks manufacturers	405
3900	Misc. manufacturing industries (SIC 3900-3999)	48,752
3911	Jewelry & precious metal manufacturers	2,887
3914	Silverware & plated ware	786
3915	Jewelers' materials & lapidary work mfrs.	936
3931	Musical instrument mfrs.	587
3942	Doll manufacturers	301
3944	Games, toys & child's vehicles manufacturers	992
3949	Sporting & athletic goods, misc. manufacturers	2,423
3951	Pen & mechanical pencil manufacturers	189
3952	Lead pencils & art sup.	321
3953	Marking device mfrs.	6,249
3955	Carbon paper & inked ribbons manufacturers	155
3961	Costume jewelry mfrs.	1,001
3962	Flowers--artificial	301
3963	Button manufacturers	151
3964	Needles, pins & other notions manufacturers	395
3991	Broom & brush mfrs.	506
3993	Sign & advertising displays manufacturers	26,466
3993A	Display designers & producers	3,010
3993B	Display fixtures & materials	791
3993C	Electric & neon sign manufacturers	19,140
3993D	Sign erectors & repairs	2,210
3993E	Nameplate makers	1,185
3993F	Sign letters & painters	1,515
3993G	Party or convention decorators	585
3995	Casket manufacturers--burial	347
3999	Manufacturing industries, misc.	4,651
3999A	Model makers	867

TRANSPORTATION, COMMUNICATION & PUBLIC UTILITIES

Total Firms		254,708
20+ employees		169,024
50+ employees		35,304
100+ employees		3,195
500+ employees		417

See PCS Transportation Index & Communication Index

SIC NO.	DESCRIPTION	QUANTITY
4000	Railroads, switching & terminal companies	3,469
4011	Railroads--line-haul operating	3,380
4100	Local & suburban passenger transportation companies (SIC 4100-4172)	25,597
4111	Local & suburban transit	2,365
4111A	Airport transportation services	2,080

SIC NO.	DESCRIPTION	QUANTITY
4119	Passenger transportation-- local, misc.	10,325
4119A	Ambulance services	4,935
4119B	Limousine services	4,805
4121	Taxicab companies	6,655
4131	Intercity highway transportation services	5,595
4142	Bus & tour charter services	4,135
4151	School bus companies	756
4171	Bus terminal services	67
4172	Motor vehicle services	27
4200	Motor freight transportation & warehousing services (SIC 4200-4231)	137,605
4212	Trucking companies-- local	27,115
4212A	Delivery services--local	7,650
4212B	Baggage transfer services	2,135
4212C	Trucking & carting-- general	14,365
4213	Over-the-road trucking companies	31,950
4213A	Mobile home transporting companies	2,095
4213B	Contract haulers	675
4213C	Trucking--heavy hauling companies	25,350
4214	Furniture moving & storage companies	12,855
4219	Trucking companies, local & long distance	50,386
4221	Farm product--storage	6,510
4221A	Grain elevators	5,805
4222	Refrigerated warehouses	2,610
4222A	Cold storage warehouses	901
4222B	Frozen food lockers	1,430
4224	Household goods warehouses	1,875
4225	General warehouses	16,860
4225C	Warehouses	15,505
4226	Special warehouses, misc.	825
4231	Motor freight terminals	869
4300	U.S. Postal service	2
4310	Post offices	30,958
4400	Water transportation companies (SIC 4400-4469)	7,318
4411	Deep sea foreign trans.	241
4420	Sea transportation firms	96
4421	Deep sea domestic trans.	34
4422	Coastwise transportation	46
4423	Intercoastal transportation	17
4431	Great Lakes transportation	15
4441	River & canal transportation	180
4450	Water transport firms	1,288
4454	Towing & tugboat services	718
4459	Water transport--local, misc.	546
4463	Marine cargo handling cos.	968
4463A	Terminals--marine	21
4469	Water transport, misc.	4,645
4469A	Marinas, yacht & boat clubs	3,220
4500	Transportation by air companies (SIC 4500-4583)	9,825
4511	Air transportation-- certified carriers	9,915
4511A	Airlines--certified	143
4511B	Airlines--noncertified	3,752
4511C	Air cargo & express packages	5,500
4521	Aircraft charter, rental & leasing--non-certified carriers	4,467

PCS MAILING LIST COMPANY
85 CONSTITUTION LANE   DANVERS, MA 01923
INSIDE OF MA 1-800-622-LIST   Fax 1-617-777-9161

CALL TOLL FREE
OUTSIDE MASSACHUSETTS
1-800-532-LIST

40

One advantage to compiled files is the price. You will be able to rent compiled names at a substantially lower cost per thousand than you would be able to rent respondent lists. And, because competition with the list owner is not a problem, you are often not expected to provide a sample mailing piece or to adhere to a certain mailing date.

f. RESPONDENT LISTS

A respondent list is a list of people who have responded to some other offer — for instance, people who subscribe to some magazine or people who have purchased a certain product similar to the product you're selling.

1. Finding a list — Direct Mail List Rates and Data

Probably the best way to find a respondent list for your particular market is to consult *Direct Mail List Rates and Data,* (DMLRD) one of several catalogs published by Standard Rates and Data Systems (SRDS). It includes literally thousands of sources for lists. No matter what you want to sell, you're guaranteed to find a potential list outlet here.

If you're serious about getting involved in direct mail, you'll want to own a copy of this catalog. An annual subscription includes six update issues and sells for around $270. While this service would keep you advised of new lists that are coming into the marketplace, initially you'll probably opt to purchase just the main volume. Later, when you determine how much you'll use this service, you can add the updates.

There are two main sections in the catalog: business lists and consumer lists. The business section includes those lists that would be used to target professionals (usually at their business address) who would be interested in buying products related to their work. The consumer section includes those lists that would be used to target consumers (usually at their home address) who would be interested in buying items of a personal, rather than professional, nature.

2. Subject/Market Index

The Subject/Market Index allows you to look up, by subject, exactly what you want. For example, you could find a list of hobbyists or model train collectors.

3. Title/List Owner Index

The Title/List Owner Index allows you to look up a list by the name of the owner or the name of the list. This would prove useful if you've heard that a certain list is available or you know who owns a list, but you don't know how to get in contact with the appropriate person. For example, you spot a copy of *Model Train Digest* in the store and you suspect that they might have a list appropriate for your market. You could then look up the correct address and contact person for that magazine in the Title/List Owner Index.

The DMLRD is a virtual fountain of information; much knowledge can be gained simply by perusing its pages. That knowledge can be enhanced by calling some of the list owners directly and asking for more specific information about their lists or by consulting a list broker who has a working under- standing of hundreds of lists and can guide you to those most likely to work for your product.

4. Understanding the DMLRD listings

Once you've found a list title that sounds like a good possi- bility, how do you interpret the specifics? It's not as complex as it looks upon first glance. Each listing contains information that you need to evaluate when making your selections. Sample #11 shows a typical listing.

(a) Personnel

Here you'll find the name of the broker or representative you should contact about the list. This is the person who is directly responsible for this specific list. You don't have to contact this person, however, if you're working with another independent

SAMPLE #11
DIRECT MAIL LIST RATES AND DATA

	Total Number	Price per/M
Buyers (1985)	14,216	70.00
1964	9,262	*
1983	8,758	85.00
Recipients (1984-85)	23,496	50.00
Inquiries (1984-85)	6,015	*

Selections: key coding, 1.00/M extra; state, SCF, 3.00/M extra; ZIP Code, 5.00/M extra.
Minimum order 5,000.

6. METHOD OF ADDRESSING
4-up Cheshire labels. Pressure sensitive labels, 5.00/M extra. Magnetic tape (9T 1600 BPI), 15.00 fee.

8. RESTRICTIONS
Two sample mailing pieces required for approval.

SWEET ENERGY

Media Code 3 536 6005 4.00   Mid 627163-000
Sweet Energy.

1. PERSONNEL
List Manager
AZ List Managers, 31 River Rd., Cos Cob, CT 06807. Phone 203-829-8086.

2. DESCRIPTION
Mail order catalog buyers of dried fruit and nuts; 90% female.
Average unit of sale 26.00.

3. LIST SOURCE
20% direct mail; 80% space ads in Yankee, Country Journal, Gardeners' Marketplace.

4. QUANTITY AND RENTAL RATES
Rec'd August, 1986.

	Total Number	Price per/M
Total list (1984-85)	30,502	55.00
1985 (1st half)	7,500	60.00

Selections: recency, 5.00/M extra; state, SCF, ZIP Code, 3.00/M extra; keying, 2.00/M extra; 1985 buyers, 35.00/M.
Minimum 5,000.

5. COMMISSION, CREDIT POLICY
20% commission to recognized brokers.

6. METHOD OF ADDRESSING
4-up Cheshire labels. Pressure sensitive labels, 5.00/M extra. Magnetic tape (9T 1600 BPI), 20.00 deposit.

7. DELIVERY SCHEDULE
Two weeks from receipt of order.

8. RESTRICTIONS
Two sample mailing pieces required for approval.

11. MAINTENANCE
Cleaned and updated regularly.

TEXAS YA-HOO CAKE COMPANY

Media Code 3 536 6246 1.00   Mid 630163-000
The Original Texas Ya-Hoo Cake Co.

1. PERSONNEL
List Manager
Names in The Mail, Inc., 10710 Shiloh Rd., Dallas, TX 75226. Phone 214-661-5701.

2. DESCRIPTION
Mail order buyers and recipients of cakes, cookies, candies, jellies, etc.; 70% female.
Average unit of sale 48.00.

3. LIST SOURCE
Direct mail.

4. QUANTITY AND RENTAL RATES
Rec'd September, 1986.

	Total Number	Price per/M
Buyers (1985-86) (No. 1269)	18,870	80.00
Recipients (1985-86)	53,495	60.00

Selections: state, SCF, 2.50/M extra; ZIP Code, 5.00/M extra; key coding, 1.00/M extra.
Minimum order 5,000.

5. COMMISSION, CREDIT POLICY
Orders cancelled after mail date require full payment.

6. METHOD OF ADDRESSING
4-up Cheshire labels. Pressure sensitive labels, 6.50/M extra. Magnetic tape, 15.00 nonreturnable fee.

8. RESTRICTIONS
Sample mailing piece required for approval.

3M CONTEMPORARY COOKING SERIES

Media Code 3 536 6267 7.00   Mid 636003-000
3M Company.

1. PERSONNEL
List Manager
Qualified Lists Corp., 135 Bedford Rd., Armonk, NY 10504. Phone 212-324-8900.

2. DESCRIPTION
Members of a cookbook continuity club; mostly women.
Average unit of sale 9.90 per volume.
ZIP Coded in numerical sequence 100%.
Selections available: ZIP tape, Nth name.

3. LIST SOURCE
Direct mail.

4. QUANTITY AND RENTAL RATES
Rec'd October, 1985.

	Total Number	Price per/M
Total list	53,966	50.00

Selections: credit cards, state, SCF, 2.50/M extra; ZIP Code, 5.00/M extra; key coding, 1.50/M extra.
Minimum order 5,000.

Direct Mail - Consumer Lists

broker. Any broker has access to the same lists and could act as intermediary for you.

(b) Description

Here you'll find out more about the list and what type of people are on it. For instance, the listing for the Texas Ya-Hoo Cake Company tells you that these people are "Mail order buyers and recipients of cakes, cookies, candies, jellies, etc.," and that 70% of them are female. You also learn that their average unit of purchase is $48.

This tells you a great deal. You know that these people have —

(a) purchased these types of foods through the mail, and

(b) spent an average of $48.

Unit of sale is important as a frame of reference for your own marketing efforts. For example, if you're selling a product for between $10 and $50, this list might be a good prospect. However, if your food product sells for $150, these people might not be very receptive.

You also want to make sure you're mailing to the decision-maker. If you're selling a book on accounting procedures, you want your piece to get into the hands of the accountant, not the office manager.

(c) List source

Here you find out how these names came to be on this particular list. In this case they came from direct mail. This tells you that they are amenable to direct mail efforts and would probably be responsive to your offer as well. Another common source of names that you'll find in the DMLRD is "space ads." These are people who have seen an advertisement in a magazine and called or written for more information or have made a purchase. These are still responsive names but perhaps not as responsive as those who can be identified as direct mail purchasers.

(d) Quantity and rental rates

Here's where you find out how much you're going to pay. (In chapter 10 we'll discuss ways of determining whether or not a certain list will be cost effective for you.) The cost depends on how many names are available and how much you will pay per thousand.

In this case, there are a total of 18,870 names of buyers, for which you would pay $80 per thousand, and 53,495 names of recipients (those who have received these goodies as gifts from their friends) for which you would pay $60 per thousand. If you were to purchase the entire list of buyers, you would pay about $1,510 (18,870/1,000 x 80) for all of these names.

There are two important things to note here:

(a) Always re-check counts before you order.

> Publishing timelines being what they are, these numbers are outdated as soon as you get your new edition of the catalog. You wouldn't want to place an order for a "complete list," thinking it will be approximately 19,000 names, only to receive 30,000 names in the mail with a bill for $2,400.

(b) Be warned that this price is only a base charge.

> There will be additional charges for the various selects you choose.

Each list contains more than simply names and addresses, and this additional information allows you to make more well-defined selections of whom you will mail to. As you get more and more specific about your choices, you'll pay a bit more for the names but you'll be mailing to fewer and potentially more responsive names.

The selections available to you, along with their associated cost per thousand, are listed in this section. In the listing in Sample #5, you can select by state, SCF (Sectional Center Facility, indicated by the first 3 digits of the zip code), zip code, and key code. The key code is the code that you assign to the list so you can track where your responses come from (See chapter 10 for more about coding and tracking.)

When selecting by SCF, you can refer to zip code maps that are available from the post office (see sample #12).

Other common selections include:

- sex,
- age,
- SIC (Standard Industrial Classification),
- title,
- size of business,
- household income,
- unit of purchase, and
- date of purchase.

In this section, you will also find the minimum order number, if any. In this case, it is 5,000. No, you can't just order 100 to see how it goes. You can, however, order 5,000 names and mail as many or few of these names as you like. Also, see section **(i)** below for information on test mailings.

(e) Commission, credit policy

This section tells you some specific information about payment and broker commissions. In the case of the Texas Ya-Hoo listing, all you learn is that if you cancel your order after your specified mail date you must still pay for the list. In other cases, you may learn such things as what the broker's commission is and when payment is due — "within 30 days of mail date," for instance.

(f) Method of addressing

Here you learn about the available list formats. The format you choose will depend on how you plan to affix the labels. Chances are you'll be using an outside mailing house. You'll

SAMPLE #12
ZIP CODE MAP

want to check with them before ordering, to determine what type of label you should provide them with.

The most common is 4-up Cheshire labels. This is simply a format where four names and addresses are listed horizontally across a page of computer paper. These labels are affixed by a standard labeling machine. Other formats include pressure sensitive or "sticky" labels and magnetic tape. Sticky labels can be affixed directly to the mailing by using the gummed side or they can be cut and affixed by a labeling machine and the customer can be instructed to peel off the label and affix it to the order form.

(g) Delivery schedule

This particular listing does not include this item. What this section would tell you is how soon you could plan to receive your list after you place your order.

(h) Restrictions

Under restrictions the most common information you'll find is "sample mailing piece required for approval." This means that the owner of the list wants to know what kind of promotion you'll be sending to their customers. You don't need to send an actual printed version of your mailing and may very well not have one available at the time you're ordering the list. What you need to send is the copy or written version of the promotion, including information on what are you selling, how much it costs, etc.

Other restrictions might include "mailing date must be approved and adhered to," "not available to fundraisers," etc.

(i) Test arrangement

Mailers will seldom order an entire list without testing the response to a segment of it first. This section will tell you what the minimum order requirement is and other particulars about special test orders.

(j) Letter shop services

In some cases, the same company that is renting a list also provides a number of other services that you might be interested in. This section will tell you what those services are.

(k) Maintenance

All lists need to be maintained on a regular basis to assure that the names and addresses are current and deliverable. Some lists are "cleaner" than others. Here you'll find out such things as how frequently the list is cleaned and what percentage of duplication the list contains.

g. CHOOSING LISTS

Choosing the right lists for your direct-mail campaign is a crucial step. A large part of the success of your efforts will rest on whether you mail to the right people.

Let's take a look at how you might choose compiled and respondent lists for your mailings.

1. Getting started

Suppose you're starting a business selling computer supplies. You've developed a catalog and now want to mail it to some prospects to see what kind of response you'll get. Where do you start?

The first thing you would do is to make a list of the type(s) of people who would be most likely to order your products. In this case, your list might include the following:

(a) Businesses with computers

(b) People who have computers at home

(c) Schools with computers

This is, however, a very broad list. If this was as far as you went in classifying your potential market, you could conceivably mail to every business and school!

How can you get more specific? By doing some research in the DMLRD. Under section 608 (Video and Home Computers) you would find over 13 pages of possible list sources for your mailings. Naturally, you can't use them all or even select test segments from them all. You need to read through each listing to determine which are the most appropriate to your needs.

Let's look at an example. Suppose you're selling computer software for household budgeting. Your selling price is around $50. As you browse through the listings in DMLRD, you notice listings for compiled files of computer owners, subscribers to various computer magazines, and purchasers of videocassettes. None of these seem quite right for your needs. Then you spot a listing for Beagle Bros. Apple Software Buyers.

This is a list of "buyers of Apple-compatible computer software packages — mostly men." The average unit of sale is $50, the list totals 86,265 and sells for $60/m or you can purchase the hotline names which total 15,000 for $70/m. Selections are available for state, SCF, and year of purchase.

You're just getting into the business, so you don't want to mail all 86,000 names. Hotline names can be good prospects, so you decide that you'd be interested in a test segment of 5,000 and you want to key code the labels so you can track response. The cost for keycoding is $1/m.

But what's this? Running charges are an additional $6/m. This shows you why it's important to read the fine print. Your actual cost per thousand for this list will be $77/m, not $70/m as you might have originally thought. You may decide that this is still a reasonable price or you may decide to go back through the listings to see if anything else strikes you as a good possibility.

2. Is cheaper better?

When picking and choosing among lists, keep in mind that a lower priced list may not necessarily be your best bet. Postage is usually the highest expense for any direct mailer, so it is better to mail to a few really good prospects than to do a blanket mailing to thousands of people who may not be interested in what you offer.

For example, if you were selling a new type of flea control product, you might consider two lists — a short list from a magazine for pet owners and a long list from a general family magazine. The pet-owners list costs $75 per thousand and the general list $50 per thousand. You might calculate that, yes, everyone who subscribes to a magazine for pet owners has a dog or cat, and is an excellent prospect, but you estimate at least 65 percent of those who subscribe to a family magazine probably also own pets and would be good prospects. So, taking into consideration the extra cost of the more specific list, you might conclude that the cheaper, more general list is the better buy. Wrong! This calculation leaves out the cost of postage. When you figure in the cost of postage (not to mention the cost of your printed materials) for those 35% uninterested parties on the general list, the more specific list is quite likely to turn out the better bet. Make sure you do your homework carefully before choosing a list.

3. Be informed

Knowing the right things to look for in the DMLRD listings and the right questions to ask can mean the difference between a successful mailing and a dismal failure. Following are some important things to consider before making the decision to rent a particular list.

(a) Source of the names

Is the list compiled from various sources, comprised of respondents to other direct mail efforts who have made a purchase, or made up of inquirers (people who have asked for additional information but have not made a purchase)? Be aware as you're reading list descriptions that not all lists contain names of actual people. Some contain only titles and company names. This may or may not be what you're looking for. Make sure you know what you're ordering.

(b) How often is the file updated?

You want the cleanest list you can get with addresses that are current and deliverable. Some files are updated only once a year. No list is going to be 100% deliverable, but, considering the mobility of today's society (moving at the rate of 15% and more each year!), an annual update means a high percentage of undeliverable. Quarterly is better and most common. Monthly is best.

You'll also want to know how it's updated. Is it updated at the source, meaning that the list owner updates addresses on an interactive basis as orders are entered and address changes are received? Or, is it updated mechanically using some of the software available through the post office or other avenues?

(c) How old are the names?

When you're renting a list from a business that's been around for several years, it's not inconceivable that many of the names on that list are old — these people haven't placed a new order for quite some time. You'll want to know what that time period is. Generally, any name that's been inactive for more than three years isn't worth renting.

When ordering subscribers to various publications be certain that you're renting active subscribers and not expirees. You want to be getting the names of the people who are demonstrating their willingness to spend money on products similar to yours. The closer in time you can capture these people (e.g., while they are currently receiving a publication or within a few months after they've placed an order), the better your response will be.

(d) Are "hotline names" available?

Hotline names are respondents who have replied to a direct mail effort in the recent past. These names are often available in three-month, six-month, and one-year selections. They will be more responsive than older names on the same list. If they're available, they're often priced at a higher rate. This higher rate is well worth it, however, for the added response you'll achieve.

(e) What other offers have been mailed to this list and what offers have been mailed more than once?

Answers to these questions will give you a basis for comparing your offer with other offers that have proven successful. If nobody else selling your type of product has used the list with any success, it's unlikely that you'll break this trend.

(f) What selections are available?

While selections are listed in the SRDS and on the data card, there may have been new additions to this list that you'll want to be aware of or different sorts that are possible but weren't included because demand for those selects isn't high. Don't be afraid to ask.

(g) What is the minimum order?

When you first use a list you'll be testing a segment of it. Minimums are usually 3,000 or 5,000 names. Again, though, you needn't mail the entire segment you receive just because you've ordered it.

When testing a list you should also ask if the names you receive can be marked. Then, if you do schedule a roll-out of the test, you won't be remailing the same test names again.

(h) What are the addressing and label format alternatives?

Make sure you know what format the list you're getting will be in so that it will work with the equipment at your lettershop. If you're having the list key coded, make sure you specify where the code should be located.

(i) Is a sample mailing piece required?

With most compiled lists a sample piece is not necessary. Owners of respondent lists, however, want to know what kinds of mailings are being sent to their customers so they can guard against what they consider to be objectionable mailings to their customers, and so they can keep competitors from mailing competitive promotions at the same time they'll be doing a mailing.

(j) When can I expect the list?

You'll be expected to provide your mail date to the list owner, but you'll want to receive the list a week or two before that mail date just in case it's not what you wanted or it's delayed for some reason. Always order your lists well in advance so you can avoid the added costs of express delivery.

h. ORDERING LISTS

When you have made your choice and are ready to order, there is certain standard information you will need to provide:

(a) The name of your company — the list owner wants to know who is responsible for the mailing.

(b) Your offer — indicate what you're selling and, in most cases, provide a sample mail piece.

(c) Your mail date — make this date as specific as possible. Most list owners will expect that you adhere to it. If for some reason you can't, you'll need to request permission to mail on a different date.

(d) Exactly which names you want — if you don't want to mail outside the country you are in, make sure you request that you be given labels for that country only.

SAMPLE #13
LIST RENTAL ORDER

p⊘i PROFESSIONAL
EDUCATION SYSTEMS, INC.
.

LIST RENTAL ORDER

Professional Education Systems, Inc.
P.O. Box 1428, 200 Spring Street
Eau Claire, WI 54702
(715) 836-9700

Order/Job #	Order Date	Req. Delivery Date

TO:_____
_____
_____
_____
_____

Ship to: Professional Education Systems, Inc.
P.O. Box 1428, 200 Spring Street
Eau Claire, WI 54702

ATTN: Mailing List Department

Bill to: Same as above

Quantity	List Description	Price Enclosed ☐

Special Instructions:

Split test_____

Omit: ☐ Canadian ☐ Foreign ☐ Military

Key Code Labels _____

Furnish in Zip Code sequence unless noted otherwise:
☐ 4-up cheshire
☐ Pressure sensitive
☐ Magnetic tape
☐ Sample mailing piece enclosed
☐ Other _____
_____

If there are any questions about the data on this Rental Order, please advise
   ☐ **Ellie Goss** or
   ☐ **Kathi Pophal**
Otherwise it is assumed that the data on this order is correct. Professional Education Systems, Inc., agrees that the list will be used only once as specified and will not be copied.

Mail date: _____

Offer: _____

Program Title:_____

Program Date, Location: _____

Authorized Signature: _____

If you want to make more finite geographic selections, make sure your specifications are clear.

(e) The quantity of names you're ordering and the price as you understand it — including added charges for selections and key codes.

(f) Your requested delivery date — be sure to include shipping instructions.

(g) A written confirmation — while most list orders are placed via phone, it's important for you to provide a written confirmation of exactly what you ordered. Then, if what you receive isn't correct, you have documentation available.

i. WHEN YOUR LIST ARRIVES

When your list arrives you'll want to check it over before you send it on to the lettershop. A quick visual check is all that's needed. You should check for the following:

(a) *Proper format.* If you requested four-up Cheshire but received 1-up pressure sensitive labels, you've got an obvious problem.

(b) *Key code.* Placement and accuracy of the key code you requested.

(c) *Address format and accuracy.* Are all elements of the address present? Are zip codes correct and in proper sequence? Do these names look like the type of people you've ordered? If you've ordered a list of doctor's offices and you see company names like "Dave's Pet Supplies," something's wrong.

(d) *Accurate count.* Make sure you received the number of names you requested and were invoiced for. You don't need to count every label — a quickly calculated estimate will suffice.

5

BUILDING A HOUSE FILE

One of the most valuable assets you have as a direct mailer is your customer file, made up of the names, addresses, and other vital information you choose to keep about each person that does business with you.

Why is it so important? Because once you "buy" a customer (and you buy that customer through the advertising dollars you spend to entice him or her to make a purchase from you), his or her name becomes your property and in its future earning potential lies value. Someone who has already purchased from you is more likely to purchase from you in the future. So your own customer mailing list should always be your first choice for a direct mail campaign and you should make a concerted effort to create, maintain, and use a customer list.

Are you making the best use of your customer file? Do you —

(a) Know who your past customers are?

(b) Make use of follow-up sales promotions?

(c) Keep an active prospect list?

(d) Have a means of identifying recent purchasers and purchasers of specific products?

If not, you're not making the best use of your customer and prospect names, and you could be losing thousands of dollars each year.

a. WHAT IS DATA BASE MARKETING?

A data base is nothing more than a collection of data about a group of related "things." In the case of direct mail marketing, the "things" you will be concerned about are your customers. Your data base will be, in essence, a sophisticated customer list.

A simple form of data base would be a collection of file cards in a file box. The collection of cards and the information contained on the cards is a type of data base. Of course, today, a data base is far more likely to be maintained on a computer than in a filing box.

The beauty of the computer lies in its ability to retrieve data from the records it contains quickly and in many different combinations — much more quickly and effectively than you could ever do it manually. All the information you maintain on your customers will be in your data base and, because of the way you and the computer have organized that data, you'll be able to retrieve it in a wide variety of useful forms, such as mailing lists, management reports, billing statements, etc.

A data base is built slowly. You'll test it, expand it, and rearrange it until you find a system that will be as flexible and efficient as you need it to be.

The mere creation of a data base doesn't automatically launch you into the world of data base marketing, however. Before you can do that, you need to develop an organized system for managing all of that data. This means coming up with ways to organize it, update and maintain it, and retrieve and manipulate it.

Data base marketing is a relatively simple marketing concept. In fact many direct marketers already operate a data base marketing system of sorts. Data base marketing is simply marketing centering on the manipulation and use of data from the data base.

b. WHAT DATA BASE MARKETING CAN DO FOR YOU

1. Benefits

Data base marketing has a number of benefits to offer:

(a) Increased productivity — you'll save time by automating many of the tasks that you currently handle manually: e.g., generation of mailing lists, preparation of sales reports, various accounting functions, etc.

(b) Quick retrieval — names and addresses can be sorted by various characteristics.

(c) Automated generation of commonly used business forms — for example, invoices, statements, form letters, accounting reports, etc., can all be generated with customer names and addresses neatly in place.

(d) Collection and analysis of marketing information — speedy information on such things as how many customers purchased the ABC product at $x vs. $y or how many customers have purchased five or more items.

By maintaining a data base you will be able to describe your customer list in terms of recentness, frequency, value, type of product purchased, or any other characteristic you choose to collect, enter, and maintain. This is valuable marketing information — information that even some of the smallest companies can take advantage of in one form or another.

2. Cross-selling

The importance of this information can be quickly and easily demonstrated through cross-selling. Cross-selling involves selling an item to a customer who has purchased a similar item in the past.

Suppose you market seminars. You recently developed an advanced ceramics seminar as a follow-up to your basic ceramics program. With your data base you will be able to easily request a list of all those people who attended your basic ceramics class. You can then do a special mailing to these people telling them about your upcoming advanced course. You not only save money by not mailing to all of the customers on your list, but you're able to prepare a very personalized mailing — a mailing that is guaranteed to get a better response than a general program announcement would.

3. Develop a customer profile

Perhaps one of the most interesting applications of data base marketing is the ability to "profile" your customers. Depending on the information you maintain, you will be able to eventually put together a typical customer profile that will aid you immeasurably as you go out and prospect for new customers.

For instance, suppose your data base tells you that your typical customer is —

- female,

- between the ages of 35-45,

- married,

- has two children, and

- her typical purchases are household items between $15 and $35.

You can now search for lists of people with these characteristics.

The larger your customer base or the more complex your products and services, the more likely that setting up a customer data base on computer will be appropriate for you.

The benefits of your data base are virtually limitless, but these benefits are dependent on your creativity, forethought, and organization. Remember, what you put in is what you'll be able to get out. No more.

c. CREATING A DATA BASE

1. What data should you keep?

Before you can even begin to set up a data base you need to thoroughly examine your needs. Put these needs in writing and be as specific as possible, but don't attempt to take this task on by yourself. Ask for input.

The kind of input you need to develop a successful data base can come from three important sources:

(a) People who will need to have access to the data base (e.g., clerical help, accounting, personnel, etc.),

(b) People who will rely on your output to perform their jobs (e.g., a mailing house who will want labels to be printed in a specific way), and

(c) People who have developed data bases of their own and can warn you about potential pitfalls and make helpful time-saving suggestions based on their own experience.

Spend some time speaking to people from each of these groups, asking for their "wish lists" of what they would like the data base to be able to do and what type of information they think you should collect.

Of course, there's no end to the amount of information that you could store in your data base. As always, though, financial considerations come into play. You need to be able to separate "nice to know" from "need to know."

For example, if you're running a mail-order business you need to know the addresses and purchase history of your customers. It might be nice to know some demographic information about these customers (birthdate, number of people in the household, etc.) However, the cost of gathering, inputting, and maintaining this information might not make it worth your while to capture it in the first place. These are the kind of decisions you will have to make for yourself based on your budget and your future marketing goals.

Here are some items that are often included in customer data bases:

(a) Name, address, telephone number (and now FAX number),

(b) Purchase history (including dates of purchases, units purchased, type of purchase, monetary value of purchase),

(c) Source of sale (e.g., response to a direct mail brochure, response to a space advertisement, word of mouth, direct salesperson, retail outlet, etc.),

(d) Credit information, and

(e) Type of purchase (e.g., sports clothing vs. formal apparel).

You might also decide to set up an inquiry file, a prospect file, or a gift-recipient file in addition to your actual customer file. These names would be prospects for future sales even though they have not actually purchased from you in the past.

Once you have decided what information should go into your data base, you need to ensure it is accurate, current, and complete. Let's take a look at what it takes to meet each of these requirements.

2. Accuracy

The accuracy of the information in your data base is dependent both on the people you hire to do order entry and file maintenance and on the instructions you give them.

Accuracy and speed (in that order) should be prerequisites in hiring personnel to work with your customer file. All candidates should be thoroughly tested and given clear instructions as to what their position will entail. After employees are hired, their performance should be monitored regularly and checks should be in place so work can be spot-checked and errors can be identified.

It's important that management have in place a set of standards for data entry people to rely on when entering data. Guidelines should be given for how information is entered, what information is needed, and what to do if that information is not readily available.

For instance, it is common for direct mailers to track response based on coding which appears on the order form or the mailing label. This coding allows responses to be analyzed and helps management make decisions about what lists to use in the future, identify copy or design that worked or didn't work, etc. For the data entry people, it is important that this code always be located in the same place and be of a consistent format (for instance, a three-character alpha-numeric code). If this code is not on the order form or the mailing label is missing, data entry people need to have clear standards regarding what they should do.

It's a good idea to establish a detailed order entry manual for your company that includes directions on address entry and address corrections and on what to do in certain specific situations (e.g., wrong price, use of P.O. box vs. street address, storage/maintenance of "shipped to" vs. "billed" name and address). Consistency is important — remember the old computer motto, "garbage in, garbage out." Take steps to ensure that no garbage is going into your data base.

One important aspect of maintaining an accurate and efficient data base is the avoidance of record duplication and the removal of duplicate names when they are discovered. Duplicate records can happen quite innocently. For instance, you have a "John Smith" responding to mailing A and a "J. Howard Smith" responding to mailing B. Is this the same person? How can you tell? One way is by using address and phone number as a means of identifying potential duplicates.

Caution must be exercised, however, and decisions must be made as you balance the need for a duplicate-free list (and the marketing dollars such a list will save you) against the possible elimination of a unique record. For instance, in the previous example, even if the records for "John Smith" and "J. Howard Smith" have the same address and phone number and seem like duplicates, you can't really be sure that they aren't two separate people. The "J". could stand for "Jeffrey" or they could be father and son.

The standards you develop for your data entry staff will have to take these kinds of situations into account and decisions will have to be made up front about whether you want to err on the side of having too many duplicates or too many unnecessary record deletions.

The format you choose for data storage will also affect the amount of duplication you have in your file.

A common name and address format is as follows:

- Line 1: Full first name, middle initial, and last name,

- Line 2: Company or organization,

- Line 3: Street number and name, building or apartment, and

- Line 4: City, state or province, and zip code or postal code.

If the order of the first two lines were reversed, a merge/purge would not identify a duplication between the following list items:

- John Smith
  XYZ Company
  1111 Standard Rd.
  Anytown, USA/Canada, and

- XYZ Company
  John Smith
  1111 Standard Rd.
  Anytown, USA/Canada.

3. Currentness

A customer calls to tell you that his or her address is changing. An "address correction requested" mailing is returned to you with new information. A customer requests to be removed from your mailing list.

Each of these situations requires action on your part. Each requires that you change the information you have in your file. Remember, your data base is only as good as the information it contains. You lose money when you allow that information to become dated.

Let's consider a simple example. You have 10,000 names in your customer file and you mail the entire file once a month. Of these 10,000 names, 10% are dated — the customer has changed address, changed jobs, asked to be taken off your list, hasn't responded to a mailing in over three years, etc. What does this mean? It means that each month you send out 1,000 pieces of mail that do not reach a potential customer. If your average cost per piece is 30¢, you are throwing away $300 a month — that's $3600 a year! Nobody can afford to throw away money. Make sure that your list is kept up-to-date. Make address correction and deletion of old, inaccurate records a priority for the people maintaining your mailing list.

Keep your list "clean." Old names do nothing more than take up space. If a customer hasn't responded for quite some time, you need to jostle their memory and ask them if they want to stay on your mailing list. You should schedule a regular (perhaps semi-annual) mailing to customers who haven't been "active" for ____ months. The mailing could be on the order of "we want you back ... if we don't hear from you by _____, we'll be forced to remove your name from our mailing list." Include a promotion for a new product with the mailing to help defray some of the costs. Remove the names of non-respondents and update the history of those who do respond.

Another way of keeping your file current is to include a statement such as "Has your address changed? Please provide us with your new address" on all order forms. Many mailers also periodically send mailings with "address correction requested" language on them so that the post office will provide them with the corrected address for customers or businesses that have changed address. There is a charge for this service based on the pieces returned to you.

4. Completeness

You will also want your data base to be complete. At the outset you'll want to make sure that provisions have been made (fields are available) to enter all the information you will need to draw upon in the future. If a certain element of this information needs to be accessed as a unique unit, make sure that it is not contained in the same field as other bits of information.

The answer to the question of "what information do I want to keep on each customer?" depends on both your marketing approach and the capability of your computer system. (If you don't own a computer, the answer to this question can depend on how much time you or one of your employees has to devote to manually maintaining a list).

5. Pitfalls to avoid

There are a number of pitfalls to avoid as you contemplate the development of a data base marketing system. First and foremost is failing to gather enough information in advance. The importance of good communication cannot be emphasized enough. Make sure that you know what your needs are now and have a good idea of what they will be in the future.

Make sure that everyone who will be using the system for information, for work output, or for data entry has had the opportunity for input. Make sure you develop a system that can coordinate all the varied needs of your company into an efficiently operating data base.

The second most important pitfall to avoid is sloppy maintenance of information. The information you pull from your data base will lose its value quickly if it's incorrectly entered or sloppily maintained.

Here are some additional pitfalls to avoid:

(a) Data fields which are too small, especially in the name and address areas.

(b) Data which is not maintained in separate fields. One company combined first and last name into one field and later found that it would be impossible to send out personalized letters to customers which read "Dear Bill:" instead of "Dear Bill Smith."

(c) No allowance for changes in the future. Don't paint yourself into a corner with your data base. Make sure, for instance, that you've left flexibility for the addition of fields at a later date.

d. CREATING A PROSPECT FILE

1. Customers vs. prospects

There are two distinct segments to your house file — the customer segment and the prospect segment. We all have a good idea of what a customer is — it's someone who has purchased a product or service from your company. A customer is the person who makes the buying decision, not, necessarily, the person who pays for the product. For example, if you market seminars for secretaries, the secretary is your customer (assuming that he or she chooses the seminar), even though it is the boss or the company that actually pays for it.

A prospect, on the other hand, is somebody who has expressed an interest in your product or service, or somebody who you think would be interested in your product or service.

For example, you send out a brochure advertising your line of garden tools. Someone calls to ask about your products, but doesn't make a purchase. That's a prospect and you want to make sure you obtain their name and address so you can send them information on your products in the future. They have already expressed an interest in you; you know they are a hot potential customer. You want to make sure you can get in touch with that person in the future.

Here's another, less obvious, example of a prospect. You sell cheese boxes, and most of your customers purchase these cheese boxes, not for themselves, but for friends and relatives. The customer is the person who makes the decision to purchase — in this case, the person giving the gift of cheese. The person receiving the cheese, however, becomes an important prospect for future mailings. They are already familiar with your product and are likely to buy from you in the future. The boss in the secretaries' seminar example above would be another example of a prospect: someone who is familiar with your product but has not yet made a purchase decision.

2. The prospect file

When you rent a list from another company you are renting a list of people you feel will be prospects for your product offering. You can also compile your own list of prospects which you can mail again and again with no rental charge.

Your prospect list is a list of those people who, for some reason, you feel may some day become customers. You may feel this way because they've expressed an interest in your products or services, because they have been referred to you by a current customer, or because you know they have interests that indicate they may be potential customers.

The type of information you will want to keep on prospects is very similar to the information you'll maintain on customers and includes —

(a) name,

(b) address,

(c) telephone, and

(d) how or why they were added to your list.

Suppose an ad you placed for a certain product generated a number of responses from people who were interested. You coded this ad "C2" and entered the name, address, and phone number of each person that called in response to the ad. Later you decide to do a mailing offering these people a special discount on this product if they order by a certain date. You would certainly want to be able to retrieve those names from your computer (or manual system). Since you've used a special code (C2), you'll easily be able to do this.

When a prospect makes a purchase decision, wonderful! You can now add this name to your customer list and remove it from your prospect list. If your data base program cannot make this transfer automatically, you may need to physically go through each list on a regular basis (perhaps quarterly) to update both files. This would involve checking each name on the prospect list to see if it shows up on the customer list as well. If it does, delete it from the prospect list. This procedure helps you assure accuracy in your mailings. It also gives you some indication how successful you have been at turning prospects into customers.

3. Capturing names for your prospect file

As a direct marketer you need to capture names whenever and wherever you can. Names mean money. Every time you can add a name to your list, whether it's a customer name or a prospect name, you're adding the potential for a future sale.

Marketers use many creative ways to capture prospect names. In fact, you've probably fallen prey to many of these techniques without even being aware of it. Every time you mail in a coupon for a product rebate, every time you request information about some product or service, every time you send for a free product sample, your name and address is being entered into somebody's prospect file.

There are countless ways to capture names and this is where your creativity can come into play. Following are some suggestions to get you started:

(a) If you run ads in newspapers or magazines, always include a coupon or response device of some sort that requires a name, address, and phone number. The response may simply be "for more information." This not only helps you build your prospect list, it also helps you track the responsiveness of your space advertisements.

(b) Ask for referrals. Offer incentives to customers who can "get a friend to…"

(c) Keep an eye out for lists that are in the public domain. These may include association rosters, directories, even telephone listings. How can you tell if they're in the public domain? Look for a copyright indication. If there is none, and no indication that the names belong to someone, you are free to enter them into your computer. Always remember to include some coding to indicate where they were obtained.

(d) Non-respondent labels. Suppose you do a mailing and responses start to come in. You notice that, in some instances, the person placing an order is not the same person that appears on the label. You're free to enter both names into your computer — the customer and the prospect. Be aware, though, that the reason the prospect didn't respond could be that they're no longer at that address.

(e) "Send information." Mailings aren't just for generating orders. You can capture additional prospect names by including a blank on your order form that says, "No, I don't want to order now, but send me more information on...," or "No, I don't want to order now, but add me to your mailing list."

(f) Evaluation forms. Evaluation forms serve two purposes: they give you an indication of what your customers think of your products and they allow you to gather additional information about your customers. If you request (and get) the customer name, you can append this information to the information already in that customer's file or, if it is a new name, add that name to either the prospect file or the customer file.

(g) Surveys. Surveys are a good way to collect information on potential and existing customers. The additional demographic information you collect can be added to your computer files (assuming the fields are available) and can be used as a way of further defining your market base.

e. FILE ENHANCEMENTS

Another way to collect information on customers that gets into a bit more complex aspect of data base development is data base enhancement. You match your customer file against another, similar, file and append or add information that you don't currently have.

For instance, suppose your file contains only name, address, phone, and purchase history. You learn that one of your primary sources of mailing lists (and hence the source of a great percentage of your own customers) has information in their file on size of family, ages of children, yearly income, etc. You'd like to include that data in your file because it would help you make more exact selections of lists when you are promoting particular products. So, if you come out with a line of casual clothing for children in the pre-teenage bracket and you can identify those customers on your file with children in this age range, you will be quite sure that you'll get a good response from this segment of your file.

Also, by learning more about who your customers are, you're in a better position to rent lists from other companies. Identifying the traits and characteristics of the customers on your file is known as *profiling*. Searching for these same traits and characteristics on other files is called *cloning*. The more you know about your customers, the easier it is to go out and find prospects with similar characteristics. These prospects will yield high response rates for your future mailings.

It can be time-consuming and expensive to develop your own enhanced data base, but it can be done. By surveying your customer file, asking questions over the phone, encouraging salespeople and others to pass on any information they obtain, and adding that information to your file, you can eventually develop a detailed collection of information on your customers. Or, you can look into the commercial marketing data bases and consider appending the information contained there to the information you already have in your file.

The type of information you keep in your files is limited only by your imagination (and computer space!). The more information you gather, the more knowledge you will have about your customers. The more knowledge you gain about your current customers, the better you are able to go out and prospect for new customers.

Developing an extensive customer file will allow you to —

(a) Speak to your customers as individuals and address their needs specifically, and

(b) Save money. When you do a mailing of a catalog advertising garden tools, for instance, you will be able to mail only to those people who have purchased garden tools in the past.

f.   RENTING YOUR LIST

Once you've built your customer list up to a respectable size, (generally at least 15,000 names), you can consider renting your own list to other mailers. Many companies make a good profit at doing this and find it a very easy and inexpensive way to generate revenue.

There are three prerequisites to renting your list:

(a) Adequate size — You must have a list of adequate size to make it attractive to other mailers. While list owners with lists of less than 25,000 total names may still find marketers interested in renting their names, lists smaller than this don't provide a great deal of potential in terms of rollouts.

(b) Product affinity — You must have a list of purchasers of a product, or group of products, that has an affinity for the products of other marketers.

(c) Segmented list — You must be able to segment your list in ways that make it attractive and useful to other marketers. For instance, they will want to select by recentness of purchase, dollar value of purchase, geographic area, sex, etc. If you aren't able to offer these types of selects, your list will not be very attractive to other mailers.

Not all list owners make their lists available for rental. As we've said, your list of customer names is a very valuable commodity and some mailers consider it too valuable to make it available to others.

1. The list manager

Unless you, or somebody in your organization, has an extensive knowledge of all of the facets of marketing mailing lists, your first consideration should be finding a list manager to handle all of the details for you.

Hiring a list manager is similar to hiring any other kind of employee or consultant. The first step you should take is to make it known that you are looking for a list manager. You can do this by contacting other direct mailers you know and asking them some questions about their list manager:

(a) Are they pleased with the service they receive?

(b) Are they pleased with the number of rentals they receive?

(c) What don't they like about their list manager's service?

Another way of learning about list managers is to read trade magazines and attend trade conferences. Many managers rent booths at conferences where you can speak to them about their services and their interest in representing your list.

Then contact some of the managers you're most interested in and invite them to your place of business to discuss how they would work with you in the rental of your list. Spend some time in advance developing a list of questions to ask prospective managers:

(a) How will you market my file?

(b) Where do you advertise?

(c) What trade shows do you exhibit at?

(d) What other companies have you represented?

(e) What segments do you feel you would offer from my file?

(f) What price do you think you could charge for this list?

Once you're selected a list manager, you'll be asked to sign a contract, usually for a one- or two-year period.

Your list manager will then take care of all of the details of promoting and selling your list, including billing and collecting money owed. Your list manager will also be instrumental in determining what price to charge for your list (per thousand names — e.g., $80/m) and determining how to segment your list to make it most useful to other mailers. He or she will also probably help you find a service bureau to physically house your file and run the lists for customer use (unless your own computer is powerful enough and you have the personnel in-house to do this on your own).

2. Your role

Your primary role in the list rental process is to approve rental requests as they come in. Your list manager will forward requests to you for your approval when other companies want to rent your names. These requests will be accompanied by information on who the mailer is, what segment of your list is being requested, when the mailing is scheduled, and what the offer is. You should also receive a sample of the mailing piece that will be used. Based on all this information, you will have to determine if the product offered competes with anything you're currently promoting or if it's a product that you don't want promoted to your customers.

You will also be asked to submit updates to your list on a regular basis so that it is up-to-date and includes new customers and corrected addresses, etc.

3. How much money will you make?

On a regular basis (usually monthly) you should receive reports from your list manager indicating rental activity for your file — who has rented, what they've rented, what they have been charged, when they were billed, and if they have paid.

The cost to you of renting your list is two-fold. You will pay a commission to your list manager and you will pay a processing charge to the list bureau you use. There will also be a broker's commission deducted from your payment when a company other than the one you're working with rents your list.

These charges, however, are not "out-of-pocket" costs in that you will not actually be writing checks to the list manager or service bureau. Charges are simply deducted from the revenue you receive.

How much can you expect to make from list rental sales? It's always very difficult to predict accurately (be wary of list managers who profess to be able to do this), but, in very general terms, you can expect to turn your list approximately ten times a year. This means that if your list consists of 25,000 names, you can expect to rent 250,000 names every year. Keep in mind, however, that the first year or so your rental income will be slow in coming as the marketplace becomes familiar with your list, tests are run, and rollouts begin to be scheduled.

4. List security

In the past, list owners protected their lists against unauthorized use by "seeding" the list with decoy names — names of people who were actually employees or acquaintances of the company, not customers. They would then receive a copy of any mailing that went out to their list and compare this mailing piece to their list of authorized mailings.

However, with more sophisticated computer systems and increased segmentation, this method may no longer be adequate. Savvy mailers may detect (and eliminate) your decoy names or, through very finite selections (specifically

SCFs for instance) your decoys may not be pulled from your file.

While seeding your file with decoy names is still a good idea, you might also consider using commercial tracking systems such as U.S. Monitor or MultiSafe that track list users for you.

g. LIST EXCHANGES

As the price of lists goes up, more and more mailers are taking up the practice of exchanging names with each other. Suppose you're selling ceramic pottery supplies through the mail and have 200,000 customer names in your file. You become familiar with another company that sells similar hobby supplies whose list rents for $90/m on the market. You'd like to mail that list, but don't think you can afford the steep price. What do you do? Ask about a list exchange.

The benefits of exchanging names with another company are obvious — you reduce your costs and you're often allowed to make more specific selections than would be available through regular channels.

The drawbacks? Many mailers are hesitant to exchange with competitors for fear of cutting their own throats. Others prefer to rent their lists to take advantage of the often substantial revenue that renting can bring in.

6

DEVELOPING YOUR PROMOTIONAL FORMAT

A product to sell. A list of potential buyers. These are two key elements in embarking on a direct mail campaign. But there is a third: a direct mail package.

The classic direct mail package consists of a letter, a brochure, and a response card (or BRC — business reply card), inserted in a #10 envelope. This isn't, by any means, however, the only mailing format you can use to achieve successful results. In fact, the possibilities are endless.

a. SO YOU THINK YOU'VE SEEN EVERYTHING

As more and more direct marketers compete for the same marketing dollars, and for the attention of consumers amidst growing piles of "junk" mail, mailing formats have expanded beyond the traditional brochure or letter.

The main reason direct mailers turn to these unique formats is to make their sales message stand out from the myriad of other messages bombarding their potential customers each day. If your package gets noticed, the theory goes, it will get opened and read.

Another important function of these packages is getting past the notorious "gatekeepers" — particularly in the business-to-business marketplace. The gatekeepers, either the personnel in the mailroom or the secretaries, are the people who decide whether to pass the mail along to its intended receiver or to relegate it to the circular file. Hence, direct marketers have created packages that look like official government mail, packages that look like federal express deliveries, packages that contain plastic "charge-cards," packages that make use of striking holograms, and a variety of other unique ploys to get attention — and, ultimately, an order.

Let's take a look at some of these techniques.

1. Videotape

No longer do marketers have to rely on a simple two-dimensional brochure to sell their product. Today, videotape makes it possible for potential customers to see (in their home or office) a three-dimensional, active presentation of a sales message. Whether used for a product demonstration, an infomercial, or a fashion show, video can help direct marketers make their products "come alive." And, with the development of relatively inexpensive disposable cardboard videotape packaging, they can do it at a fraction of the cost of sending traditional videocassettes through the mail.

2. Product samples

Sending product samples through the mail is an old practice. It is done primarily to entice customers into the stores to purchase "the real thing." We've all received these small packages containing soap, shampoo, a food item, or some other product. And, most of us go to the effort of opening and using these samples. What a great way to use the mail to literally get your product into the hands of your potential customers!

3. Dimensional packaging

Champion International recently used a unique packaging concept to introduce a new paper product. Their agency developed a nine-part mailing based around a miniature pool set complete with a cue stick, pool balls, chalk, and rack. Some of the various headlines on the boxes read, "Now you can exceed your reach..." or "When it's time to get the ball rolling..."

The Network of City Business Journals used a bright orange 13" x 9½" x 21" box to promote advertising in their journals to media buyers during the Halloween season. The outside of the box was boldly printed in black type — "Want to put some spirit in your media plan?" Inside the box, recipients found a twin-size white sheet that had been converted into a ghost costume by cutting three round holes for eyes and nose. The advertising message was printed on the sheet.

Dimensional packaging can go beyond form. Structural Graphics, in cooperation with Electronic Speech Systems, has developed a new type of dimensional advertising — print that speaks. More complex than ads that play simple tunes, MailCall (the name for the new technology) can actually mimic individual voices and sounds!

4.   Computer diskette

Electronic brochures are animated marketing programs distributed on diskette. With these electronic brochures, prospects not only receive information, they can also participate in the sales message by selecting options from various menus. This is truly interactive marketing.

5.   Fax

The growing use of fax machines in offices everywhere has opened up a new avenue for marketers to reach their markets. Fax is quick, it's direct and, since it is still a relative novelty in many offices, it gets attention.

Now, instead of trusting your advertising message to third class mail delivery (which could take one to two weeks to reach its mark), you can get your message to a potential customer in a matter of seconds.

The only problem is that, as with telemarketing, a few unscrupulous marketers have caused the use of fax for the delivery of unsolicited advertising messages to be closely scrutinized by authorities. In fact, 13 states have passed laws restricting (not yet prohibiting) unsolicited faxes. Other states may follow suit. What most marketers are finding is that, while fax is a responsive means of direct advertising, it does tend to antagonize a number of potential customers. Those who like it, like it, those who don't … well, it's currently one of the most controversial means of getting a sales message across.

Fax can even work both ways, as Johnnie Walker is discovering. Their newest billboards, instead of giving an 800-number, feature the line "Fax me at ###-###-####, if you drink Johnnie Walker Red" next to their attention-getting graphics. Faxes are answered by return fax within 24 hours.

b. CHOOSING A FORMAT

The above techniques are innovative and you should keep such creative ideas in view, but when starting out in direct mail, you will probably want to stick with more traditional formats. Traditional doesn't have to mean boring, however. If you have many products, you might choose to develop a catalog or a card pack. If you have several products, but not enough for a catalog, you might choose to develop a brochure that could be mailed alone without an envelope (a self-mailer). If you have just one product you wish to promote, you might also use a self-mailer or you might decide to simply mail a letter in a #10 envelope.

Your choice of mailing format will be determined by —

(a) the product or products you are selling,

(b) your budget, and

(c) your market.

For example, suppose you're selling a line of clothing designed for pregnant women. The product— clothing — demands four-color treatment. It's difficult to portray clothing in black and white in such a way that it will convince customers to order. Photography, design, and layout will be important as you promote this type of product.

Your budget may dictate that you can't afford a 64-page full-color catalog. So, you may decide to develop an initial campaign which consists of a 22" x 34" self-mailer, folded to an 8½" x 11" mailing size, highlighting a number of your most promising items.

Your market will be pregnant women, perhaps in the age range of 25-40. Since they will be concerned about their appearance, four-color is a must as are well-done photos of attractive models wearing the clothes you've designed. A full-color catalog or brochure would be your format of choice instead of, for instance, a letter.

On the other hand, if you have self-published a book on "How to Be A Good Manager," your format options would be greater (and less expensive).

Your product, a book, doesn't have to be portrayed in four-color, or even two-color, to encourage a potential customer to make a purchase decision. Your budget will be a major factor in making a decision of what format to use (as will testing, which we'll discuss in a later chapter). Your market, businesspeople, is accustomed to receiving direct mail promotions for books and other educational materials that run the gamut from full-color catalogs to simple letters.

When selling "high-ticket" items, make sure your mailing piece represents the quality of your product — use four-color, glossy stock, large formats.

Don't forget to consider your envelope. In business-to-business mailings, plain business envelopes work well. With consumers, though, it's a good idea to include "teaser copy" on the envelope.

c. GETTING HELP

When you're first starting a direct mail effort, you'll want to save money wherever you can — wherever it's most feasible to do so, and it's quite possible that, at least initially, you could produce your own direct mailings with basic office equipment.

Later, you could expand your efforts through the many desktop publishing systems available that allow people with no formal design training to prepare mailings that are attractive and effective.

Ultimately, however, as you move into more complicated mailing pieces, you will want to consider the use of outside services. Freelance copywriters and designers abound and print shops often provide useful services.

A bonus to working with a freelancer is that, in working with someone outside your field, you'll pick up some tricks of their trade that you can then use in your own work.

1. Choosing freelancers

An option that many small businesses choose is working with an outside agency or freelance talent, at least temporarily. But how can you make an informed choice when you're looking for outside help? Here are some tips for deciding exactly what you need and choosing the agency or freelancer that will be right for you:

(a) Look around

What ads, billboards, or brochures have attracted your attention? Where were they done? Who did the design, writing, and production? By checking into these sources further you'll have a list of talent you can pursue.

As you're looking, you should be mindful of the style used in these ads. If your company has a sedate image, you won't want to work with advertisers known for their flamboyant style.

(b) Ask your colleagues

How are your colleagues having their advertising materials produced? Who have they used and what results have they obtained? Were they horrified, dissatisfied, satisfied, or elated with the finished product? Were deadlines met? Would they use the same service again?

(c) Look for someone with experience in your business

The best agency or freelancer will be one that's already worked for others in your same business. They'll already have background knowledge they can draw from and you'll save time in briefing them on your product as well as being more confident that the finished product will be acceptable.

(d) Shop around

Just as when you're hiring a new employee for your company, choosing outside advertising services should be a careful process. You'll want to interview a number of people, check references, and look at samples carefully before making your choice.

Here are some additional questions that can help you make the decision. Does the agency or freelancer you're considering —

(a) share your view of the customer,

(b) understand the problem you're attempting to address,

(c) understand your business, and

(d) understand you?

Your final gauge of the effectiveness of your choice will be based on how well you're able to communicate with the outside service people, how closely the ads fit your company image and, most importantly, the response to the ads that are developed. A finished advertisement may look marvelous, but if it doesn't generate response, it's worthless.

2. Working with freelancers

Regardless how good the person you're working with is, if you're not able to communicate effectively with him or her, your advertising is destined to fail. You need to be open, honest, and thorough when explaining a project and reviewing completed work. Here are some tips for working effectively with outside help:

(a) Talk about price up front. Get a written estimate that spells out what is to be done and when, when money will be paid, what circumstances would result in additional charges, what happens if you're not satisfied with the work, etc.

(b) Provide ample information. Product specs and samples, your thoughts on how you want the material presented, news releases, articles, etc. The more information you can provide, the happier you'll be with the completed piece.

(c) Be available to answer questions, review artwork, etc.

(d) Be open to new ideas. Don't interfere. Don't tell your freelancers how to do their job. That's what you're paying them for.

(e) However, don't be afraid to speak up if they're way off base. Be constructive in your criticism, and *don't nitpick*.

(f) Don't change your mind or throw monkey wrenches into the process. Remember, you're paying based on your original description of the work. Changes not only frustrate the people you're working with — they add to the cost of the piece.

When working with freelancers, the question of ownership of the finished work will likely arise. Businesses that work with independent consultants (freelancers) own (hold copyright) to the work created only if they have a written agreement stating that these rights have been transferred from the freelancer.

If the person creating the work is a member of your staff, however, and the work was completed during the course of employment, you own all of the rights to the work.

d. WORKING WITH PRINTERS

While you can certainly use a copy machine to reproduce simple letters for small mailings, when you're dealing with quantities in excess of 100, it's more economical to go to a commercial printer.

The best advice about using printers is to become familiar with the printers in your area and learn what's available.

Then ask them what kind of work they have done in the past? Ask to see samples and then speak to the people who have used their services to find out if they were satisfied with the service, quality of the work, and the price. Find out about the prices that various printers are charging and the lead time they ask for when working on jobs.

1. Getting bids

To make sure you're getting the most for your money, solicit bids for each job you're having printed. For this purpose, it is useful to draw up a form with spaces you can use to fill in the job specifications (e.g., quantity, design features, type of paper, colors of ink, packing and shipping instructions, date quotation needed). You can mail the form or call the printer and give them the specifications. When you get bids back you can determine where to go for the best price and quality.

Should you tell the losing bidders the difference between their bid and the winning bid? Yes. Give them a percentage that they were over on the job. Should you give them the opportunity to meet or better the winning bid? No. Generally, it's recommended that you don't. Why? Because word is likely to get out that you went beyond the regular bidding process to obtain a lower price and, in the future, other printers will adjust their prices (up!) in anticipation of your call. Simply thank the losing bidders for the bid and tell them you'll be sure to include them in the bidding process for your next job.

Once you've received a formal bid make sure that each and every aspect of the job (from beginning to end) is included. Make sure that charges for such things as plates, film, and freight are itemized. You should have the printer you choose put the accepted bid in writing and you should then follow up with a purchase order that indicates the agreed-upon charges for the project. Request that any adjustments to the original bid be submitted in writing. This will make your life a lot easier when you receive the final bill and will help avoid unnecessary disputes.

2. Saving money on printing

There are a number of ways that you can save money getting your material printed. Again, perhaps the best way is to develop a good working relationship with the printers in your area. They can give you a valuable education on the printing process and inform you about their needs and how you can conform your jobs to those needs to reduce costs. Also, keep the following suggestions in mind:

- Select the right printer and the right printing process. Certain jobs are best suited for certain presses and can be done more economically if they're done on the right equipment.

- Gang your print jobs. This simply involves combining two or more jobs for a single press run and is a great way to save money.

- Be aware of trim waste. Whenever you schedule a print job, make sure that you're making the most effective use of the full sheet size for that press. However, sometimes there will be waste. Consider other uses that you could put that extra space to such as memo pads, routing slips, etc.

- Consider the use of colored paper to give a two-color effect when you're just using one color of ink.

- Look into the use of stock printed material. Many suppliers offer a variety of preprinted, colorful bulletins, etc. that are very economical for short runs.

- When choosing ink color, select those colors which are offered by your printer as "standards." Mixing inks for special colors will add substantial cost to your print job.

- Avoid bleeds (areas where printing runs off the edge of the paper). These are more difficult for the printer to print and, consequently, add to the cost of your job.

- Check with printers to see if they have leftover stock from prior jobs. If they do, and it will work for your job, cost savings can be substantial

3. **Additional tips for working with printers**

- Proofread and double check everything before you send your artwork to the printer. Sample #14 shows a proofreading checklist. Any changes that you make after the proofing process are considered "author alterations" (AAs), and you will be charged for them.

- Determine your mail date and then work backwards from that date to schedule due dates for creative, copy, art, type, printing, folding, labeling, and insertion.

Proofreading Checklist

COPY

Product description correct and consistent _____
Price correct and consistent _____
Headlines correct _____
Photos captioned_____
Numbering correct throughout _____
Correct apostrophes and quotation marks _____
Logo included _____
Correct fax, telephone number and address _____
Spelling check (bottom to top) _____
Company name and address on all parts of promotion_____

ORDER FORM

Title on form _____
Source code _____
Item code _____
Discount correct _____
Guarantee included _____
Credit card information & signature _____
Delivery time indicated_____
Shipping and tax information _____
Company names and address on order form_____
Thank-you included _____

_____   _____
Signature   Date

Final boards proofed: _____
                            Date

A proofing checklist such as this one allows you to:

- provide a structured checkpoint for all promotional materials before they go to the printer
- establish accountability/quality control should errors occur

The items on your list will vary according to your internal policies and the product you sell.

Build extra time into your schedule for the unexpected and always ask to receive your job at least a week earlier than you actually need it. When speaking to printers and getting quotes, make sure to ask how much time they need to do the job and get time commitments in writing.

If you anticipate a late delivery, ask your printer to send partial shipments of the work so you can at least get started on the mailing.

- Make sure your instructions (and those of your graphic designer) are clear. This will avoid errors and the need to make revisions after the proof stage; giving the printer a complete dummy of your job can also be very helpful.

- To help avoid delays (and keep costs down!) use standard paper and envelope sizes.

- Various parts of your job may best be handled by different printers. Shop around to make sure you're getting the best quality as well as the best price.

- If you're unhappy with the job (if it hasn't met your specs, if your proof changes weren't made, if the print quality is poor, or if the job was delivered late), talk to the printer and ask for a reprint or an adjustment to your bill — the standard compensation rate is between 10 and 15% of the total bill.

- Ask that any negatives or artwork sent to the printer be returned with the finished job. If you don't ask it's generally accepted practice that these items stay with the printer.

- Make sure that you see proofs of all jobs. With a one- or two-color job, a blueline proof is sufficient. If the job is more complicated, ask to see a color key proof. While this won't show you a true representation of the color, it will show the color breaks. It's the printer's responsibility to match your proofs, so it should not be necessary to ask for a press proof in addition to the bluelines. This will only delay the job and may add additional cost.

7

THE DIRECT-MAIL LETTER

Direct-mail letters are easy to prepare and extremely cost-effective when compared to even the most simple brochure. There are no design costs, no typesetting charges, and minimal printing costs. (Depending on the quantity, you can even successfully reproduce letters on your office copier!)

The most important aspect of the direct-mail letter is the copy. But even the preparation of sales-oriented, persuasive copy can be mastered by someone within your organization, saving you the cost of paying a freelance copywriter (or adding one to your staff).

Let's take a look at the steps to preparing effective, direct-mail letters.

a. FOCUSSING IN

1. Identify your audience

No matter what type of promotion you're using, identification of the target audience is a crucial first step. Will you be mailing to your current customers? Which current customers? What sets this group of customers apart from your entire customer base?

- Have they all purchased a similar product in the past?

- Have they all made a purchase within the past six months?

- Have they all spent a minimum dollar amount of $____?

- Are they all relatively new customers?

If you're using a rented list, the same strategy applies. Who are the people on this list? The rented list is more than a collection of names and addresses; it represents a group of people — prospects for your product. What do you know about them? Are they male or female? How old are they? What is their disposable income? How often do they buy through the mail?

2. Define your offer

Once you've chosen a group of people to market to, you need to identify your offer as precisely and clearly as possible. Before you can begin to write the direct-mail letter, you need to clearly understand the main point you're trying to make.

Don't complicate the offer by trying to sell everything and anything you possibly can. A letter that attempts to sell a dealership as well as equipment *and* offers a free catalog will be confusing to the reader and will likely be thrown away before a response decision can be made.

If you're attempting to generate inquiries for a new line of products, limit your offer to inquiry generation. Don't muddy the waters by attempting to gain a few immediate sales of other products as well. Direct-mail letters work best when the offer is simple, easy to understand, and clearly presented. By successfully targeting a select list and presenting a clear offer, you can obtain returns in excess of 5%, and that's pretty good in direct mail.

b. WRITING A SUCCESSFUL DIRECT-MAIL LETTER

1. Outline your letter

Once you've determined the market and composed your offer, the next step is to outline the letter. Proceed from point A to points B, C, D, etc., in a logical manner, and you're less likely to lose your audience. A typical organizational structure for a simple direct-mail letter might be the following:

(a) Here's what we have to offer.

(b) Here's why we know you'll be interested.

(c) Here are the benefits you'll gain by responding now.

(d) Here's how you order.

(e) P.S. — here's what we have to offer.

Sample #15 is a typical direct-mail letter.

As you can see, successful direct-mail letters work in a circular manner. If the offer you've outlined in the headline and repeated in the body copy is somehow overlooked, you want your prospects to pick up that same bit of information in the P.S. — the second-most-read (next to the headline) part of any letter.

As we proceed with our discussion we'll use the offer of a new product catalog as the basis for the development of a direct-mail letter. This offer will be mailed to a list of your current customers who have requested other catalogs from you in the past and who have ordered merchandise from those catalogs.

2. Compose a benefit-oriented headline

In order to effectively catch the attention of your target market, you need to offer a clear benefit as quickly as possible. The headline is the best place to do this. A benefit is a direct value for your audience. When you write a benefit headline, you don't want to make your audience "work" to infer the benefit. For instance a headline like, "XYZ Company Introduces Its New Product Catalog" requires your prospects to stop and think. What they'd probably be thinking is "so what?" and chances are you'd lose them immediately.

In writing benefits (whether they appear in a headline, body copy, or the P.S.) always remember to focus on the

SAMPLE #15
DIRECT-MAIL LETTER

Benefit Headline →

Our Personal Organizers Save You Time And Money!

Dear Executive:

Here's what we have to offer. →

We'd like to help you streamline your busy days with our acclaimed personal organizers. And, to introduce you to these valuable time management tools, we're offering a limited-time special offer on several varieties of pocket and briefcase-size designs.

Here's why we know you'll be interested →

These personal organizers are:

- Priced **right** — you'll find our organizers offer the same high quality as our competitors', but at a much more attractive price
- Designed to fit comfortably in your pocket, briefcase or handbag
- Customer tested — the people who have used our organizers over the years (our customers) have shared their suggestions for improvements with us — and we've implemented them! Here are just a few comments:

Testimonials →

"Your personal organizers are worth their weight in gold. I simply can't say enough about them! " (Susan Barnes, Nome, AK)

"Since I purchased your personal organizer I've saved at least 30% of my time — and that time means money. Your organizer has paid for itself over and over again!" (Joe Dallas, Houston, TX)

"I'd like to tell all of my friends about your personal organizers — but in today's competitive job economy, I don't want to give them an edge." (Stacy Kingster, Madison, WI)

"Thank you. Thank you. Thank you. Your personal organizers have literally saved my job." (Davey Pophal, Phoenix, AZ)

Here are the benefits you'll gain by responding now. →

You can put the power of our personal organizers to work for you too! And, when you respond now, you'll save 25% on the regular price of $54.95.

That's right. To introduce you to what we (and our customers) consider to be a powerful time management tool, we're offering you the chance to purchase a personal organize in your choice of color and style for **only $41.21**.

Here's how you order. →

To order, simply fill out and mail the enclosed postage-paid order card or call, toll, free, 1-800-333-3333. Your personal organizer will be on its way to your office within days.

Sincerely,

Ms. Very Organized

P.S. Here's what we have to offer. →

P.S. Take advantage of this limited time opportunity to purchase a personal organizer at 25% off the regular retail price!

target audience and not on yourself. In the example above, a benefit headline that would focus on the audience might be, "Don't Miss the New Products and Special Prices in Our Fall 1992 Catalog!"

3. Put your offer up front

When writing advertisements of any kind, the most important factor is keeping the prospect reading. You want to lead that prospect through the letter — you don't want attention to lag. Assuming your headline attracted attention, your prospect is now at the introduction of your body copy. To maintain your prospect's attention, you need to immediately pick up on the benefit offered in the headline and expand that benefit to focus on the offer.

In this case, your introductory paragraph might begin: "Send for the XYZ Company Fall 1992 catalog today and learn about hundreds of new products at special prices you won't believe!" You've reemphasized the benefit introduced in the headline and now you're ready to go on by providing some additional information about the catalog and its contents — you've "hooked" the reader.

4. Stick to the point

We've already seen how easy it can be to lose your reader by introducing too many variables into your offer. By sticking to the main point, you walk the reader through your letter without creating confusion. A good direct-mail letter —

(a) introduces a benefit,

(b) reinforces the benefit (as many times as necessary),

(c) asks for the order, and

(d) closes.

Any extraneous information introduced in the letter will cloud your offer, create confusion, and probably result in your letter being tossed into the nearest wastebasket.

One bit of information that is always pertinent and appropriate is testimonials from real people. Testimonials lend credibility and increase response.

5. Write with design in mind

Even though one of the benefits of using direct-mail letters over brochures is that you won't need to hire a graphic designer, design considerations do come into play as you compose your letter.

You want your letter to be visually appealing — to invite readership. One guaranteed way to discourage readership is to use long sentences and long paragraphs that begin at the left-hand margin with no indentation. Your prospects will take one look at a letter like that, see nothing but gray copy blocks and push your letter aside. Nobody wants to tackle a letter that looks like a legal document.

Your letter can be visually appealing if you use several reader-assisting techniques such as —

- short sentences,
- short paragraphs,
- indented paragraphs,
- bold and underlined phrases, and
- bulleted points (like this list).

You can even get fancy within the text of your letter by using an additional color, penciling in marginal notes to draw attention to certain phrases, circling parts of the letter, etc.

Put yourself in the reader's position as you review your completed letter. Would you be likely to read this correspondence if it crossed your desk? If not, you need to make some changes.

6. Personalize

One of the benefits of using letters in direct marketing attempts is the opportunity to personalize your sales message.

Of course, personalization is easiest to accomplish when the number to be mailed is small — you don't want to hand-sign 10,000 letters! But, if you're mailing to a small, finely targeted audience, you can personalize by —

(a) using the prospect's name in the salutation: "Dear John Smith" rather than "Dear Customer,"

(b) hand signing each letter,

(c) writing in marginal notes, or

(d) typing each envelope (rather than using mailing labels).

Personalization is just one additional way of setting your marketing attempts apart from the hundreds of mass-marketed appeals that consumers receive each year. Your missive will be much more likely to pass the "censors" (mail room staff, secretaries, and the prospect) if it looks like a "real" letter. Personalization can do the trick.

c. GETTING PAST THE CENSORS

We've already made reference to the censors that exist in any office or home setting. These are the people who make a decision on whether to pass your mail on — and the people who make a decision on whether to read your mail. A censor could be someone other than your prospect (like a secretary or spouse), or the prospect himself or herself.

Why are more and more people turning to simple letters to advertise their goods and services? Because consumers are becoming adept at recognizing advertising when they see it. Advertisers have learned that they must get past the censors in order to get their selling message across.

A boldly emblazoned envelope or flashy, four-color brochure screams "ADVERTISEMENT" and often ends up in the "circular file" with hardly a glance. A letter, however, immediately appears more personal and is more likely to be read.

8

THE DIRECT MAIL BROCHURE

While letters can serve the purpose of promoting your products adequately in many cases, there will come a time when you'd like to have a brochure for one (or more) of your products.

Start to pay close attention to the brochures and catalogs you receive in the mail, noting how layouts are arranged, how photos are used, how models contribute to the photo, what elements attract your attention, etc. You can gain a valuable education at no cost simply by learning from the techniques of others.

How do you know if these techniques work? If you see the same elements being used again and again by a certain company, you can bet that they're effective. Most companies test their mailings frequently and continue to use those brochures and catalogs that prove most effective.

The guidelines in this chapter will help you put together a polished brochure. These same guidelines will also aid you should you decide to work with a freelancer to design your brochures.

a. MAKE A ROUGH

Visualization is important when preparing a brochure, regardless of the product you're promoting. The best way to accurately visualize your brochure is to prepare what is called a rough — a rough sketch of the completed brochure indicating size, placement of type and graphics, folds, etc.

Suppose you will be working with a finished size of 8½" x 11". Use this size of paper to plan your layout, and ask yourself the following questions:

(a) How large is the space?

(b) How much copy must I have to adequately describe my product and set forth the offer?

(c) What other elements must go in the brochure (illustrations, coupons, etc.)?

b. TYPE

The choice of type might seem incidental to your piece, but it is actually a very important element in designing an effective mailer. There are virtually hundreds of typestyles or "fonts" in use. Your selection will be determined by the fonts available to you as well as by the type of product you're selling.

Type styles, or fonts, have "personalities." Those personalities should be chosen based on the personality or image you wish your product and your mailing piece to convey. For instance, if you were selling farm equipment you would not choose a flowery italic typestyle. You would want to use a strong, no-nonsense type face. Sample #16 and Sample #17 show examples of commonly used type styles and various type sizes.

Serif typestyles — the kind with the little "feet" — are the most frequently used, as most studies show that this style of type is the most readable. This book is printed in a serif type. Sans serif typestyles have no "feet." This gives them a crisp, modern look, but can make them more difficult to read, particularly in body copy.

Typesetters and printers can provide you with samples of the type they stock. These samples can be used for selecting a font appropriate for your use and for fitting type into a layout.

SAMPLE #16
COMMON TYPE STYLES

SOME COMMON TYPE STYLES OR FONTS

(COURIER)
Smith's Jogging Togs at a "No Sweat" Price!

Dear Smith Sweats Buyer:

    We wanted to let you be one of the first to know about the special sale prices on Smith's quality sportswear. For a limited time only we're offering our cotton fleece sweatshirt, sweatpants and sweatsocks at an all time low, low price.

(HELVETICA)
Smith's Jogging Togs at a "No Sweat" Price!

Dear Smith Sweats Buyer:

    We wanted to let you be one of the first to know about the special sale prices on Smith's quality sportswear. For a limited time only we're offering our cotton fleece sweatshirt, sweatpants and sweatsocks at an all time low, low price.

(NEW CENTURY SCHOOLBOOK)
Smith's Jogging Togs at a "No Sweat" Price!

Dear Smith Sweats Buyer:

    We wanted to let you be one of the first to know about the special sale prices on Smith's quality sportswear. For a limited time only we're offering our cotton fleece sweatshirt, sweatpants and sweatsocks at an all time low, low price.

(ATHENS)
Smith's Jogging Togs at a "No Sweat" Price!

Dear Smith Sweats Buyer:

    We wanted to let you be one of the first to know about the special sale prices on Smith's quality sportswear. For a limited time only we're offering our cotton fleece sweatshirt, sweatpants and sweatsocks at an all time low, low price.

(BOOKMAN)
Smith's Jogging Togs at a "No Sweat" Price!

Dear Smith Sweats Buyer:

    We wanted to let you be one of the first to know about the special sale prices on Smith's quality sportswear. For a limited time only we're offering our cotton fleece sweatshirt, sweatpants and sweatsocks at an all time low, low price.

(PALATINO)
Smith's Jogging Togs at a "No Sweat" Price!

Dear Smith Sweats Buyer:

    We wanted to let you be one of the first to know about the special sale prices on Smith's quality sportswear. For a limited time only we're offering our cotton fleece sweatshirt, sweatpants and sweatsocks at an all time low, low price.

(TIMES)
Smith's Jogging Togs at a "No Sweat" Price!

Dear Smith Sweats Buyer:

    We wanted to let you be one of the first to know about the special sale prices on Smith's quality sportswear. For a limited time only we're offering our cotton fleece sweatshirt, sweatpants and sweatsocks at an all time low, low price.

7 PT.	Smith's Jogging Togs at a "No Sweat" Price!
8 PT.	Smith's Jogging Togs at a "No Sweat" Price!
9 PT.	Smith's Jogging Togs at a "No Sweat" Price!
10 PT.	Smith's Jogging Togs at a "No Sweat" Price!
12 PT.	Smith's Jogging Togs at a "No Sweat" Price!
14 PT.	Smith's Jogging Togs at a "No Sweat"
16 PT.	Smith's Jogging Togs at a "No
18 PT.	Smith's Jogging Togs at a "No Price!
20 PT.	Smith's Jogging Togs at a Price!
24 PT.	Smith's Jogging Tog "No Sweat" Price!
30 PT.	Smith's Jogging at a "No Sweat"
36 PT.	Smith's Jog Togs at a "No

When choosing typestyles, stick to one "family" of type in any one particular piece. A type family consists of various styles that usually include a regular face, bold, and italic, and may run to condensed, light, ultra-light, demi-bold, and extended. Within one family, you can usually find enough variety to cover your needs. Mixing different families of type can result in a cluttered, amateurish piece.

Never run more than six lines in a paragraph — four is even better. The maximum number of characters you should have in one line is 66 — again, shorter is better. Vary the length of your lines and paragraphs to provide visual interest. Break up solid blocks of copy with numbered or bulleted lists, call-outs, screened boxes of copy, illustrations, etc.

Use both capitals and small letters in headlines, not all upper case, which is too difficult to read: "Closeout Sale, February 2" is easier to read than "CLOSEOUT SALE, FEBRUARY 2," particularly when working with large point sizes.

Never set type over photos. Again, it's difficult to read. Readability should always be your primary guide when selecting and arranging type.

c. COLOR

As with the choice of typestyle, the choice of color should be based on the image you wish to portray and the type of product you're selling. Pink would not usually be a good choice for men's clothing. Dark brown would not be a good choice for most women's cosmetics.

The key when choosing color for ink and paper is to present your readers with the greatest possible contrast. Black ink shows up well against almost any light background and will probably be your least expensive choice. Almost black shades of brown and blue ink are good, too. Avoid using other colors for type as they can be distracting.

The use of a second (or third) color can draw attention to your brochure, but each additional color adds expense. You'll want to check with your printer to determine the effect of your color and paper choice on the price of your finished piece.

d. PHOTOGRAPHS

Photographs are a critical element in layouts. Studies have shown that photos increase readership better than other types of graphic elements.

Always use captions with photos to highlight important selling points. This helps you to get the most impact out of your graphics and draws reader attention through your piece.

Action photos are more effective than static photos. For instance, it's better to show your product being used by a model than to just show your product alone. Product groupings where you combine a number of different products together in an attractive grouping are another effective use of photos. For instance, if you're selling cookware, you might gather an arrangement of pots and pans together for one shot. Including other appropriate elements in your photos also adds interest. Again, using the example of pots and pans, you might include various cooking utensils, food, etc.

Closeups can be used to highlight various features of your product. These closeups can be used as insets around a full product shot. If your product would benefit from it, you could use a series of photos showing a process. For example, if you're selling a craft kit, you might show the steps involved in preparing the item, illustrating how simple it is.

Generally, the larger the illustration, the better the readership. Multiple illustrations are good, too, but, again, only when they contribute to describing your product.

e. THE COVER

The cover of your brochure is what will attract your potential customers and entice them to look inside. Your cover should clearly indicate what you're selling and lead the reader into the brochure. How do you do this? By making judicious use of copy and graphics.

It's not necessary to use graphic illustrations or photos in a brochure (although studies show that these embellishments can increase response). Typestyles, borders, and other simple elements can be used to attract attention and deliver your sales message. However, if you can get a good photo of your product —one that is not distracting or amateurish in its execution — by all means use it to show the customer what you're selling.

Ask yourself —

(a) Will a headline be enough to attract attention?

(b) Is an illustration required to attract attention and/or show the product?

(c) Should there be more than one illustration?

A simple brochure cover will consist of an attention-getting headline, a graphic, and your company logo. That's really all you need to get your sales message across and, if done effectively, to get that potential customer to look inside.

Your back cover should be a version of your front cover. You don't know which side of your brochure your potential customer will be looking at first. If they happen to pick it up "backwards," you will want them to know immediately what you're selling, just as if they were to pick if up from the front.

Your back cover will also include your mailing indicia and a space for the mailing label to go if you will be mailing the brochure as a self-mailer (without an envelope).

Your order form may also appear on the back cover and be designed so the mailing label is a part of the form. This way, you will be assured that your mailing label is returned to you for tracking purposes. If you place your order form on the inside, you will need to make sure it's located so that the mailing label will be included when it's mailed back to you.

f. THE INSIDE LAYOUT

Suppose you'll be doing the obvious with your 8½" x 11" sheet of paper and folding it in half so that your surface size is 5½ "x 8½". This gives you two columns to work with for an inside layout, right?

Wrong. Regardless of where you place the fold (or folds), you can consider the full sheet as the design area. In other words, ignore the folds when considering how you will lay out your text and any graphic elements you will be using. Consider that you will be working with one solid layout space whether you fold the sheet once or twice, sideways or lengthwise. This gives you greater freedom in placing the elements of your sales message and helps you to come up with more pleasing designs.

When working with folds, make sure that you've planned your piece to open consecutively with the progress of the message and without forcing the reader to turn the piece over and over to figure out where to go next.

There are a number of graphic elements you can use to set off your copy and draw the reader through the text. Photographs (as discussed above) and other illustrations are one type of graphic element. Let's take a look at some others.

1. Screens

A "screen" can be thought of as a degree of shading from 0% (no shading) to 100% (solid black, or whatever color your ink is).

Most screens provide solid coverage of the area being screened. However, special screens are also available. For instance, a moire pattern provides shading that increases in intensity from top to bottom or from one side to the other. Wood texture, circles, spirals, etc., are other examples of the many types of screens available.

Be cautious when using screens, however, that you don't sacrifice the readability of your piece. Screens are most effectively used to highlight areas where readability is not critical. For instance, many direct mailers use screens for their order forms.

2. Borders

Borders are another effective means of highlighting portions of text to draw attention to these areas. For instance, guarantees are commonly set off by fancy borders.

Again, judicious use of borders so as not to detract from the text is a must.

3. Reverses

A reversal is an area with a solid background (black, if your ink color is black) with lettering the color of the paper stock (white, for instance). Reversals should be used in moderation, if at all, because they can hinder readability, and are best used when only a few words will be reversed out of the text.

4. White space

White space is the blank area between lines of text, between paragraphs or blocks of copy, and even between letters. Although not strictly a graphic element, white space is an important and often-ignored feature of layout. Make sure you let your copy "breathe" — don't try to cram too much type into too small an area. A reasonable amount of white space will make your brochure easier to read and less intimidating because it doesn't appear copy heavy. White space can also be a subtle way to guide the reader's eye and pull him or her into the text.

9

THE ORDER FORM

a. WHY WORRY ABOUT THE ORDER FORM?

Most direct-mail advertisers pay very little attention to their order forms. They're an afterthought — something that must be included but is considered a nuisance.

Don't make this mistake! *The order form is the most important element of your mailing.* A good order form serves three vital purposes:

(a) It elicits an order.

(b) It makes it easy for the customer to order.

(c) It simplifies order entry for you.

An order form *must* be included to close the sale. A telephone number alone will not suffice because many people simply will not pick up the phone to make a call — but they will fill out and mail an order form. The easier you make it to order, the greater your chances are of getting the order.

A good order form is the first step toward efficient order fulfillment. A clear, logically designed order form will please both your customers and your order processing people.

Your order form should include all of the information you need to know about the customer and all of the information the customer needs to know about the agreement they're entering into with your company — the agreement to order a particular product (or products) at a particular price.

The most common order device in direct mail is the business reply card (see Sample #18). It is one of the four standard pieces in the classic direct-mail package. However, to save expense, you may decide to design your order form as part of your letter (see Sample #19) or, if you use a self-mailer, the order form will be a part of the brochure itself. Regardless of what format it takes, however, the elements of the order form discussed here will remain the same.

b. STRUCTURING YOUR OFFER

"Buy one — get one free."
"Buy two for ½ price."
"Buy the first for $9.99 — get the second for 1¢."

What's the difference in the above offers? Is there a difference? Probably not to you, in the amount you'll receive from the customer. But there could be a very large perceived difference to your prospects.

The structuring of an offer is an important step in developing your direct-mail package. The wrong offer can make your entire mailing fall flat; the right one can make it soar.

Some offers are very simple: "Buy this radio for only $9.99." Others are more complex: "Buy this radio for only $9.99 when you sign up for our record club. You'll automatically be sent our selection of the month every 30 days. You'll have 10 days to review the shipment and keep or return it. In addition, you can always select from among the titles in our member catalog. Choose any selection for only $14.99. After you've made 3 purchases during your first year of membership, you'll be eligible for even greater savings!"

Even the simplest offer can be presented in a number of different ways. Your challenge, as a direct marketer, is to select the way that will be most appealing to your customers. Following are a number of different offer options you might want to consider.

SAMPLE #18
BUSINESS REPLY CARD

Sample Business Reply Card Format

YES! Please rush me your 3-piece luggage set for only $245 (a $550 value). I understand that if I'm not completely satisfied, I can return the luggage to **YOUR COMPANY, INC.** for a complete refund.

Name_____

Address _____

City_____ **State**_____ **Zip**_____

Daytime Phone_____ **Evening Phone**_____

❑ **Check enclosed** payable to Your Company, Inc.
❑ **Bill me**

Signature/Logo

Smith's Jogging Togs at a "No Sweat" Price!

Dear Smith Sweats Buyer:

We wanted to let you be one of the first to know about the special sale prices on Smith's quality sportswear. For a limited time only we're offering our cotton fleece sweatshirt, sweatpants and sweatsocks at an all time low, low price.

You'll continue to enjoy the comfort of Smith's Sweats when you take advantage of this special offer. Our sports gear offers:

√ Quality construction that **lasts longers**
√ Comfortable stretch styling
√ A broad range of color selections
√ **A money-back guarantee**

That's right. If, for any reason, you're not satisfied with a Smith product, simply return it to us and we'll refund your money promptly and cheerfully. That's our guarantee — and our promise.

And, if you take advantage of this special offer now, we will give you a special gift, ABSOLUTELY FREE with your paid purchase. You'll receive a Smith's special design "tummy-pack" — **at no extra cost!**

What have you got to lose? Order now by completing the handy order form below or calling, toll free 1-800-555-5555.

Sincerely,

Mrs. Smith

P.S. Act now to receive your **free** Smith's "tummy pack."

1. Indicate Quantity, Color and Size: A01

QTY.	ITEM	ITEM NUMBER	COLOR	SIZE (S, M, L)	PRICE EACH	TOTAL COST	
	100% COTTON FLEECE SWEATSHIRT	52664			$24.99		TOTAL ORDER $
	100% COTTON FLEECE SWEATPANTS	81064			$19.99		Shipping* $
	100% COTTON SWEATSOCKS	40366			$ 2.99		SUBTOTAL $
							Sales Tax** $
							GRAND TOTAL $

♦ SHIPPING CHARGES ARE $3.50 for the first item and $1.00 for each additional item ordered.
♦♦ Wisconsin residents add 5% state tax.

2. Indicate Method of Payment:

☐ Check enclosed payable to Smith's Sweatsuit Shop

☐ Bill me.

Credit Card Payment ☐ VISA (13–16 DIGITS) ☐ MasterCard (16 DIGITS)
Expires ____/____ ☐ American Express (15 DIGITS)

Card No. |__|__|__|__|__|__|__|__|__|__|__|__|__|__|__|__|
Signature _____

SMITH'S GUARANTEE! If you're not completely satisfied, we'll quickly (and cheerfully!) refund your money.

3. Please print.

SHIP TO: Name _____

Street Address _____

City _____ State _____ Zip _____

BILL TO: Name _____

Street Address _____

City _____ State _____ Zip _____

Day Phone # ( ) _____ Night Phone # ( ) _____

THANK YOU FOR YOUR ORDER!

1. By invitation only

This can lend an aura of exclusivity to your offer and is particularly effective when used in mailings to your customer file. "Since you purchased from us in the past, we'd like to offer you this new product at a 25% discount. This offer is only available to our past customers."

2. Limited time

You can create a sense of urgency by limiting your offer. "Respond by January 1 to take advantage of this special price" or "Quantities limited, order now!" are just two of the ways you could structure a limited time offer.

3. Get there first

"Free Widget to the First 100 People to Order." Again, this type of offer creates a sense of urgency and may give prospects that extra push they need to make a buying decision. Do you carefully police the number of people who get the free widget? Of course not. By sending a free widget with every order (for a reasonable period of time), you'll be creating good will with all of your customers because each will feel that "they won."

4. Free gift

The free gift or "premium" offer is very common. You've probably seen it in offers for book and record clubs, magazine subscriptions, etc.

What kind of gift should you offer? The best is one which is related somehow to the product itself. So, if you're selling women's clothing, you might offer a free piece of jewelry. If you're selling a book, you might offer a free booklet of tips related to the topic of the book.

5. Discounts

Discounts can be structured in a number of ways — for example, "Buy one — get one free," or "Half-price sale." Be careful, though, that you don't use discounts too often. There are two reasons for this:

(a) Offering discounts makes a statement about your product. A product which can never be purchased at a discount acquires a certain status.

(b) Customers can become accustomed to receiving discounts from you if you do it too regularly. They may come to look at your discounted prices as your "regular" prices and the effectiveness of this offer will wane.

6. Quantity discounts

"Take a 10% discount when you buy 10, a 20% discount when you buy 20."

"On orders over $100, we'll take $10 off."

"Call about quantity discounts for bulk purchases."

Carefully consider where to place your price breaks. Don't make the first break too large. You want to choose a point where it will be easy for the customer to say, "Oh, what the heck, if I add $5 more to my order, I'll get $x off."

This type of offer can help you to dramatically increase your average order size.

7. Cost per week

You've probably seen this technique often with advertisements for magazines. "Only .43¢ per week will bring you timely issues of *Our Magazine*."

Breaking down the price of your product can be especially effective if you're selling a high-ticket item with a price that might "put off" prospects. Framing it in a weekly or even monthly timeline can make the purchase decision less risky.

8. Send no money now

The easier you can make it for your customer to order, the more likely you are to get the order. How much easier could it be than to simply check a box and toss a business reply card into the mail?

If you decide to use this technique, however, monitor your returns and all the costs associated with those returns and order processing carefully. With a strong product, this technique can work very well. With a marginal product, however, you may find that the costs of handling returns (and your final back-end results) don't justify a "send no money now" offer.

9. Free Trial

"Try our product for 30 days. If it doesn't do everything we say it will do, send it back. You'll owe nothing."

The free trial offer is a good way to get your product in the hands of your customers and, because it's "free," response can be increased. As with the "send no money now" offer, however, backend response must be monitored very carefully.

10. Money back guarantee

Minimize risks for your customers by offering a generous guarantee. Ordering through the mail is risky. The customer hasn't seen the product and has only your copy and graphics, perhaps a photo, to judge the value of their purchase. If they aren't given a guarantee of their satisfaction, they may decide that the risk of ordering is too high.

In direct mail, guarantees are a must. They are by far the most important part of your offer. Don't neglect to include one!

c. DESIGNING YOUR ORDER FORM

When designing your order form, involve your order entry personnel in the development of the form. They will be able to help you lay out a form that includes all the information they will need in the order that is most efficient for data entry. Keep in mind, though, that the order form must be easy for the customer to use as well. Don't err on the side of pleasing your staff at the expense of the customer. Sample #20 shows a well-designed order form.

Place your order form in a prominent spot in your package. Don't make customers search for it — that could cause you to lose a sale.

1. Make your order form logical and orderly

An order form should be visually open and attractive and should look like an order form. Cute designs may cause confusion and may get overlooked or be unused. An order form shaped like your product (a dress, for instance) is cumbersome and difficult to cut out. Order forms are best kept traditional — rectangular or square — and, if at all possible, located on the lower right-hand side of your piece where it's easy to cut out.

Number your order form so customers can easily tell what they need to do. Make it as clear and simple as possible. It can be costly to your company to process orders where the customer hasn't provided all the necessary information or hasn't included all the necessary charges. You can use color or shading to highlight important elements of the order form.

Whenever possible, try to limit the number of options on the order form. A cramped order form discourages sales and slows down the purchase process while the prospect decides which option they prefer.

If, however, you're offering a number of different products, make sure that you list them all and include space for customers to indicate their selections. Requiring a customer to fill in a lot of information that you could just as easily have provided will not enhance your chances of receiving a positive response.

YES! I'd like to order from Smith's Spring Catalog! Please send me the following:

1. Indicate Quantity, Color and Size:

QTY.	ITEM	ITEM NUMBER	COLOR	SIZE (S, M, L)	PRICE EACH	TOTAL COST
	100% COTTON FLEECE SWEATSHIRT	52864			$24.99	
	100% COTTON FLEECE SWEATPANTS	81064			$19.99	
	100% COTTON SWEATSOCKS	42068			$2.99	

	TOTAL ORDER $
	Shipping* $
	SUBTOTAL $
	Sales Tax** $
	GRAND TOTAL $

A01

♦ SHIPPING CHARGES ARE $3.50 for the first item and $1.00 for each additional item ordered.
♦♦ Wisconsin residents add 5% state tax.
You can expect product delivery within 2 weeks of our receipt of your correctly completed order form.

2. Indicate Method of Payment:

☐ Check enclosed payable to Smith's Sweatsuit Shop

☐ Bill me.

☐ Credit Card Payment   ☐ VISA (13–16 digits)   ☐ MasterCard (16 digits)
Expires _____   ☐ American Express (15 digits)

Card No. [_____]

Signature _____

SMITH'S IRON-CLAD GUARANTEE! If you're not completely satisfied, we'll quickly (and cheerfully!) refund your money.

3. Please print.

SHIP TO: Name _____

Street Address _____

City _____ State _____ Zip _____

BILL TO: Name _____

Street Address _____

City _____ State _____ Zip _____

Day Phone # ( ) _____   Night Phone # ( ) _____

THANK YOU FOR YOUR ORDER!

Mail To: Smith's Sweatsuit Shop, 123 Main Street, Anytown, US 00000-9999
Or Call Toll-Free 1-800-555-5555.

If you simply have too many product selections to include them all (a catalog, for instance), and you must require customers to fill in information, include a one-line example to clearly indicate how information should be filled in.

2. Give all the information the customer needs

First, be sure to restate your offer on the order form as clearly and simply as possible. Begin your order form with wording that indicates a positive decision on the part of the respondent. "Yes, I would like to order..." "Please send me..." "Please rush me..." Your order form should read as though the customer is writing to you.

If you're offering a choice of terms, make sure that each choice is clearly indicated and separated and that it's clear to the respondent how to indicate his or her selection(s).

You should include an anticipated delivery time. The U.S. Federal Trade Commission (FTC) Mail Order Rule requires that when you state a delivery time in your promotion you must have a "reasonable basis" for expecting to ship within that time. If no time is indicated, you must ship within 30 days of receiving a "properly completed" order. If you are unable to meet these delivery dates (due to out-of-stock merchandise, for instance) you are required to give the customer that information along with an option to cancel their order.

Put your shipping charges on the order form and explain them clearly. There are a number of different approaches to collecting shipping and handling. The most common are the following:

(a) Weight and distance — you must provide weight information for each product in addition to a chart which the customer can use to determine distance charges.

(b) Item by item — a specific charge is indicated for each item.

(c) Flat fee — you simply state, "add $3.50 for shipping and handling."

(d) Fee per item — "Add $2.00 shipping and handling for each item ordered."

(e) Order value — "When ordering $5–50, add $___ for shipping and handling, $51–100 add $_____," etc.

Don't forget to list sales tax. Sales tax must be collected in any state where you are considered to have a "nexus" or presence. This presence could take the form of a warehouse, a salesperson, or a high degree of activity.

Be sure you include the name of your company and your address on the order form as well as each individual part of the promotion. Even if you're providing a return envelope, your name and address should be on every piece of the mailing. These individual pieces can easily be separated and you can't know which portion your respondent will hang on to.

You should always provide clear instructions for the return of products. You want to avoid the problem of products being returned without adequate identification of the purchaser.

3. Get the information you need in a form you can read

Request that information be printed on the order form. Force customers to print the information requested by providing boxes or ticked-off sections on the form for each letter/number requested. This will make it easier for data entry people to decipher names, addresses, etc. Another help to the customer is to design the order form so that it will accommodate typewriter spacing.

Ask customers to provide both daytime and evening phone numbers, indicating that they may be used if there is a question about the order. A side benefit is that you're collecting phone numbers that can be added to your customer file for possible telemarketing applications.

Request "ship to" as well as "bill to" information, especially if you sell items that are frequently purchased as gifts. This not only allows you to accurately process orders and bill the appropriate person, but gives you the opportunity to build a prospect file as well as a customer file.

Remember to code your order form on the form itself, or on the mailing label, so you can capture the tracking information you'll need to analyze response. Consider the use of peel-off mailing labels. You'll get your coding information back and you'll also have legible name and address information for your order entry personnel to read.

4. Additional tips for designing your order form

Here are some further things to keep in mind when creating your order form:

- Avoid legal-sounding terms or very formal order forms.

- List your highest priced items first.

- Consider the use of a "non-transferable" order form (one that can be used only by the person who receives the offer, because their name and address are pre-printed on the form or else the mailing label is there), as a gimmick to imply exclusivity.

- To keep your toll-free number accessible, suggest that customers fill in the order form before calling. This will save time for your phone operators.

- Add "impulse items" to the order form.

- Ask for a street address for UPS delivery.

- Date your prices and your mailers to indicate when offers expire and how long prices are valid.

- Make it clear whether your prices are in U.S. or Canadian dollars, particularly if you sell to customers in other countries.

- Don't forget to thank the customer for the order!

10

AFTER THE MAIL GOES OUT

You've planned a campaign, ordered lists, prepared a mailing piece, got it printed, folded, and mailed, and now you're ready to sit back and wait for responses to start rolling in.

Before you relax, though, schedule a post-mortem. These casual meetings allow everybody who was involved in the project to offer their input on how the process went and what could be improved. What went well? What didn't go well? What would you do differently next time? Don't wait too long to hold this meeting. You want the input while the project is still fresh in everyone's mind.

Then, when the orders are in, you can begin to look at how successful your mailing was. You need to determine if you are making money and, if you are making money, you need to know why. Was it the list? Was it the offer? Was it your copy approach? Your format?

How can you tell? Through response analysis and testing. This chapter takes a close look at analyzing the response to your mailing.

a. WHAT IS A GOOD RESPONSE?

There is no such thing as an "average" return or an average "good" return. The question most frequently asked by direct mailers, neophyte and pro alike, at direct marketing conferences every year is, "what is a good response?" The answer is that it depends on what you're selling, who you're selling to, and what price you're asking for your product. It depends on the time of year, the economy, and the whims of your prospects.

Let's look at a few simple examples to illustrate this point.

Joe Mailer sells a $350 product. He does a mailing to 10,000 people and receives 50 responses or a 0.5% return. That's terrible, you say — the response should have been at least 1%. But wait a minute. Let's take a look at what's really happening here.

- Revenue = 50 responses @ $350 each or $17,500
- Expenses = List @ 65/m or $650
- Package @ $450/m or $4500
- Total expenses 5,150
- Gross Rev. $12,350

This is more than adequate to be profitable.

So, you figure, you can make money with a 0.5% response. Again, the answer is, "Maybe you can and maybe you can't". Let's take a look at another example.

Sue Mailer sells a $15 product. She does a mailing to 10,000 people and receives 300 responses or a 3% return. "That's a terrific response!" you exclaim. But let's take a look at what this really means for Sue:

- Revenue = 300 responses @ $15 each or $4,500
- Expenses = List @ 45/m or $450
- Package @ $350/m or $3,500
- Total expenses $3,950
- Gross Rev. $550

Knowing she has an inexpensive product, Sue was more conservative with her marketing expenses. Still, she only sees a $550 gross revenue. For Sue, this was a losing proposition, even with a 3% return. And this doesn't even take into account backend, the response once returns and bad debt have been taken into consideration.

As you can see, percent response is not a determining factor in the effectiveness of a mailing. While it certainly plays a role, what counts is the cost of your product and the cost of your mailing.

How can you calculate the success of your marketing efforts? By determining your "break-even point" and measuring success as revenue in excess of that break-even point.

b. MEASURING RESPONSE

In chapter 2, we used a worksheet to predict response and estimate revenue. Once responses start coming in, you need to begin measuring the actual effectiveness of your marketing efforts.

You need to determine both where the orders are coming from (so you can tell which lists and which formats to use again) and how profitable the mailing was.

1. Where are the orders coming from?

Unlike other forms of advertising, direct mail allows you to easily tell where your responses are coming from, and thus you are able to determine which efforts were profitable and which were not.

Suppose you want to know which list of the three you used for a particular mailing provided the best response, or you simply want to know if a mailing was effective.

To get this information, you must track the responses as they come in. To most effectively track response for your mailings, you should follow these steps:

(a) Code each mailing with a unique code.

(b) Capture these codes as responses come in by either phone or mail.

(c) Record both the number of responses and the dollar volume of responses received for each code on both a daily and a cumulative basis.

(d) Measure the "half-life" for each mailing you do. This is the point at which half of your total orders for the mailing were received. It is a useful predictor of responses for future mailings.

(e) After all responses have been received and you've determined that the promotion has run its course, calculate a total response and a total revenue generated amount for each promotion.

In direct mail, it's easy to code responses. Simply place the code on the order form when mailing a letter or brochure in an envelope or on the label itself if you've designed your mailer so your label will be returned. Always make sure you've taken steps to get this coding information back. It's a simple and common mistake for mailers to remember to key code their lists but then to place the label on an outer envelope which won't be returned. If the order form on the letter isn't coded to correspond with the labels, you've lost your tracking information.

If you've coded your mailing correctly, you just have to wait for the order to come in to capture the information. Don't forget to make sure your phone operators ask for the code when a customer calls in an order. To simplify this process internally and to avoid confusion, always place the code in the same spot on the order form or label.

You can use any kind of coding system you choose, but keep it short and simple. A three-character, alpha-numeric system will provide you with virtually limitless codes. In addition to placing the codes on your mailing, be sure to keep a list of the codes you've used and what they were used for, so you can evaluate responses.

You can keep the information you get from your responses in a spreadsheet or database system which allows you to analyze the data in a number of different ways, or you can simply keep track manually. Additional columns can be added to track costs as well as revenue so that you can calculate a margin for each mailing done.

2. How profitable was the mailing?

If a mailing breaks even, it doesn't mean this was a successful mailing. It simply means that you didn't lose any money. But you didn't make any either. Sometimes, when introducing a new product or testing a new promotional format, for instance, you might expect to break even or perhaps to suffer a slight loss. That's the cost of doing business. In most cases, however, you will want to more than break even before identifying a mailing as a success.

The following two-part formula demonstrates a simple means of determining when you're making enough money to call a promotional effort successful.

The first part of the formula is:

- allowable margin (AM) – cost per response (CPR)
  = profit per response (PPR)

First, you need to consider what, for you, will be an allowable margin (AM). This is the selling price of your product less the expenses of production, packaging, and shipping. Looking back at the example of Joe Mailer, let's assume that he has calculated his allowable margin to be $195.

The next step is to determine your cost per response. Joe knows that his expenses for his 10,000 piece mailing campaign were $5,150. He also knows that he received 50 responses.

- $5150 expenses ÷ 50 responses = $103 per response.
- $195 AM – $103 CPR = $92 PPR.

The second part of the formula is:

- profit per response (PPR) ÷ money invested (MI) x 100% = return on investment (ROI)

To complete this part of the formula, Joe first needs to calculate the money invested (MI) to fill one order. This is the product cost of $350 less the allowable margin of $195, plus the cost per response of $103 for a figure of $258.

- $350 product cost – $195 allowable margin + $103 cost per response = $258 MI

So, putting that MI figure into the standard formula, we get:

- $92 PPR ÷ $258 MI x 100% = 35.65% ROI

Since this is a positive number it is an acceptable level. For every dollar spent, you made .3565 profit. Remember, you need to do more than pay for the costs of mailing your brochure and filling orders. You need to generate enough profit to cover all of your operating expenses — overhead, facilities, equipment, etc. This formula helps you determine when you're covering these costs adequately.

Since you can rarely wait for all of the results from a mailing to be tallied before you begin to plan for your next mailing, you should have some other performance indicators that you can use to help you make decisions before a campaign is completely over. These indicators can be developed over a period of time and may include —

(a) amount of mail received per day,

(b) number of returns per day,

(c) number of products shipped per day, and

(d) daily cash balances.

Without these types of internal guidelines or checkpoints, you may not be able to determine when things aren't going well and will be pulled up short later — perhaps too much later.

c. THE IMPORTANCE OF TESTING

We've seen again and again that the beauty of direct mail is in its measurability. To get the most from this measurability, you need to test, test, test.

Testing can answer questions such as the following:

- Which mailing list pulls best?
- Which offer works best?
- Which copy appeal and format generate the most sales?
- Which premium is most effective?
- Which price is the most profitable?

There are five key factors which affect response:

(a) copy,

(b) package,

(c) timing,

(d) offer, and

(e) list.

These are the major elements that you should test again and again and again. In the field of direct mail, you can never stop testing. What works today may not work tomorrow. You can't rest on your laurels. You have to continually challenge your "control" package against new packages, with your goal at all times being to maximize revenue.

Maximizing revenue can involve increasing response (whether measured by percent returned or by average order size) or decreasing expense. So, for example, you may find that a less expensive brochure will pull the same response as a more expensive package. This is maximizing revenue. Or, you may discover that one list increases response by 5% over another that costs only slightly less. A few simple calculations can tell you whether you're better off with the slightly more expensive list.

Too little testing means that you will be taking a great deal of unnecessary risk. Testing is a way of minimizing that risk by mailing smaller sample sizes to determine which list, which price, which format, etc., will work best.

Be cautious, though. Too much testing can also be a problem because it can take too much time. The marketplace is constantly changing. If you test too much before you finally go with an approach, the market may have shifted due to economic factors, competitive activity, or consumer attitudes.

The list is probably the most common variable that you will test. By taking into account some pre-testing considerations, you can reduce your mailing costs and avoid unnecessary tests. You can determine, in advance, how a list will perform based on —

(a) How closely the list matches your house file — high rates of duplication can reliably predict a higher response rate.

(b) How often your list is being used by a competitor — if your list is on the market and you notice that one of your competitors uses it often, you can assume that it's working well for that company. You can further assume that their list, in turn, will work well for you.

(c) How well similar lists have performed — you will always be seeking lists that are comprised of names similar to those on your house file or similar to those on other lists that have worked well for you. Similarly, you should avoid lists that are comprised of names which are substantially different from those

146

on your house file or on other lists that have performed well in the past.

d. HOW TO TEST

Many direct mailers (neophytes and pros alike) are put off by the prospect of testing because they don't feel they're mathematically inclined. While devising and analyzing tests does require some math skills, it basically boils down to common sense.

Testing involves doing two or more mailings of the same size that are identical except for the items being tested. The names used in each mailing must be randomly selected from the same list in order for the test to be meaningful. If you sent one mailing to 5,000 names in Utah and the other to 5,000 names in Washington, your test would be statistically invalid because any differences between the success rates could be due to the geographical difference rather than to the difference in your material. The most common way of splitting lists for testing is by odd/even zip codes. This method also prevents the problem of two people in the same office or neighborhood receiving promotions with different prices, etc.

You would use the following steps in conducting a test mailing.

1. Determine what you want to test

Test every mailing you do in some meaningful way. If you don't test, you learn nothing. All you know is that this one time, this particular package pulled this particular response from this particular list — that's all. But, had you split the list and tested some significant element of your mailing, you would have learned something.

Price, offer, list, and package format are the most meaningful variables to test. Don't waste your time and money testing the impact of one color against another or conducting tests simply to settle internal disagreements.

When testing price, test both above and below the price you've identified as the "right" price.

Incidentally, testing price can create some special problems for your administrative staff. Here's how many direct mailers handle the billing questions: if orders received are lower than the price set after the test response, they are filled at the price used in the test; if the final price is set at a lower rate than the prices in the test, customers are billed at the lower rate (or refunded to that level).

You can test more than one variable at a time by using grid or matrix testing. Grid or matrix testing allows you to test several variables at once while still maintaining a statistically valid test sample.

Suppose you want to test price and copy approach. You develop two different letters and have two different price points you want to test.

Price	Copy A	Copy B	Total
$75	6,000	6,000	12,000
$105	6,000	6,000	12,000
	12,000	12,000	24,000

All you need to do when developing your grid is to make sure that each column's total equals your required test sample size (which you've obtained from testing charts or through your own calculations).

Note that this matrix method of testing can save you money. By using a matrix in this example, your total mailing size is 24,000. If you had tested each element separately, you would have had to mail 48,000 pieces to have a statistically reliable sample size.

Always test against a control. Once a new package outpulls the control over a series of tests (perhaps 3 to 5), the test package becomes the new control and you will begin testing new formats until that control is beaten.

Never retire a successful control until a test has beaten it. No matter how tired you are of looking at the same letter or brochure over and over again, what you like really doesn't matter. It's how your customers respond that counts. Never change any element of your control package without testing the effect of that change first.

Always determine your "go/no go" response before you analyze results. This assures that your decision will be based on data and not emotion.

For instance, suppose you're testing what you consider to be a wonderful new package against your old standard. The results come in even. You decide, "Well, since they're even, I guess we'll just go with the new package." That's not a good decision.

Before you conduct the test you should determine at what point you will change packages (e.g., if there is more than a 10 percent difference in response).

2. Decide on the list, the sample size, and how names will be selected

When testing, unless you're testing list response, you should use a list that has worked for you in the past, so as to be sure of an adequate number of responses from each segment to make the test valid.

You should test enough names to receive a valid response — one that will adequately predict future performance. The size of the sample you select has nothing to do with the size of the universe you're selecting from. It has everything to do with the number of responses you expect to receive. If you're mailing 10,000 pieces and you receive 30 responses, you won't be as confident in the results you obtain as you will if you receive 1,000 responses.

As a rule of thumb, you can consider that the average direct-mail test requires between 40 and 50 responses for statistical validity. So, if you're mailing two test segments of

10,000 names each (and remember that your test segments must be of equal size), you would need to receive between .4% and .5% return to achieve the 40-50 responses needed for each segment mailed. You might decide that this level of response is so certain that you could reduce the number of pieces you mail. If you typically receive at least a 1% response to this type of mailing and you're confident that you will achieve at least that level, you would only need to mail 5,000 names for each test segment to generate a valid response.

If you want to be more precise in your selection of test segments, you could use "direct-mail testing" tables which will tell you, at various confidence levels and anticipated response patterns, how many names you need to mail to obtain a reliable sample. The Direct Marketing Association makes these tables available and you may also find them at your local library. (For the address of the DMA, see the Appendix.)

When asking for test segments, select based on the last two digits of the zip code rather than on an "nth name" basis (e.g., every second name, or every tenth name). Here's why:

(a) More mailers offer zip sorts than nth selects. In fact, many computer bureaus simply can't provide selections on an nth name basis.

(b) By using the last two digits of the zip code for your test, you get a reasonable cross section of the file and, when you go back to the file, you can easily eliminate those names you've already mailed by suppressing the same two-digit zip selections.

(c) You can't tell by visually inspecting a list whether you do, indeed, have an nth name select. You can, however, tell immediately if you've received the correct zip sort segments.

Always test segments of large lists, but don't bother testing lists of 10,000 names or less — simply mail the entire list.

Consider the following approach when testing a very large list: first test 5% of the list; if that works, test another 20%; if that still proves cost effective, roll out to the entire list.

Test in small geographic areas to take advantage of postal savings. The greater concentration of names you have within one zip code area, the lower your postage costs will be.

3. Code each package so you can measure response from each test segment

You could code the mailing label, in which case you would instruct the broker to include the code on the label. Make sure, however, that your label is placed in such a way on the order vehicle that it is returned to you and that telephone operators are aware of the test and know they should ask the customer for the code from the label when taking orders over the phone. If you will not be getting your label back (e.g., your order card will be part of a package that's enclosed in an envelope and the label will be on the outer envelope), you will need to apply the code directly to the order vehicle during the printing process. In either case, make sure your mail house knows which package goes with which list. When doing a test, it's best to supervise the initial set-up of your mailing so you can ensure that everything is done correctly.

4. Analyze responses

Analyze test responses as you would for any mailing, comparing the response from Package A with the response for Package B. Always measure results based on cost as well as percent returned. One package may outpull another by a significant margin, but if that package costs substantially more to mail, the difference may not justify changing formats.

In a price test, for example, you may receive more replies at the lower price. However, the total revenue from the higher priced package may significantly exceed that of the lower priced package. In this case, the higher price would become your new control.

The same considerations apply when testing format. A more expensive format may pull more responses. But the incremental increase in responses may not outweigh the added cost of producing the package, and the lower-priced package may actually be more cost effective to produce. Your analysis should always be based on bottom-line results.

When analyzing test results, make sure to analyze based on rollout costs, not the test costs. Why? Because your test quantities will cost you more in the mail (e.g., it costs more, per piece, to print 5,000 brochures than to print 50,000).

When testing, make sure that each test segment has its own individual source code so that response can be accurately measured. Keep thorough and clear records of your testing history.

Whether you're analyzing a test or any other mailing, don't be misled by front-end results. One company that offered videotapes through direct mail tested two offers. The first: "Send no money now. Order this tape on 30-day trial approval." The second: "Order now by sending us your check or charge order. We guarantee your satisfaction and will issue you a complete refund at your request."

Pleasantly surprised by the much higher response to the first offer, the company rolled out that offer to its entire customer file. Unfortunately, they had failed to take into consideration back-end response. After returns started rolling in, they found to their dismay that the first offer didn't, in the final analysis, outpull after all. In fact, the second offer, while it generated fewer front-end orders, resulted in a much higher "stick-rate" and was ultimately the more profitable of the two offers.

Another consideration to keep in mind is that rollouts do not usually perform as well as test mailings.

You mailed 5,000 names from a 50,000 mailing list and received a 3% response which, with your mailing and product costs, resulted in a huge profit. You decide to roll out the list and project a 3% response from the entire mailing.

Stop right there.

It is statistically unlikely. Why? Here's how Ed Burnett explains this phenomenon in his excellent book *The Complete Direct Mail List Handbook*. "It is likely, from a statistical point of view, that regression of continuing bites of a given list tends toward the mean figure. The lists that are continued are not those that are average or below average, but always the ones that do best. These tests may well be above the mean response that would have been recorded if the entire list, rather than a test segment, had been run. Thus, the rollout tends to move toward that mean figure which has a good likelihood of being lower within statistical probability, than initial test results."

The bottom line? Don't be too optimistic in your prediction of how a rollout will perform. Always anticipate that the rollout will come in at a slightly lower response level than the test.

5.   Use your mailing's "half-life" to predict response

You've devised a test and you're now anxiously waiting for results to come in so you can roll out the winner and rake in the bucks. But, unfortunately, the entire process of testing, from creation of the mailing package and selection of the lists, through analysis of the final responses from customers can take up to six months.

- You don't want to wait that long — not only because you're anxious to increase your revenues, but because you know that market conditions change constantly.

- The results of your test may no longer be valid by the time you've waited for all the results to be in to prepare a rollout mailing.

What can you do? You can determine the "half-life" for your mailings and use this figure as a way of predicting final response.

By constantly monitoring responses and building up information over a period of time you can develop an average of how many days after you receive your first response through the mail you typically have *half* of the total responses you will receive. Once you are confident in this measure you can use this "magic number" to measure response to your mailings at less than half the time it would take to wait for all responses to come in. (You'll find that you receive half of your total responses in a relatively short time.)

You can then begin plans to roll out the "winning" package, list, or offer immediately.

Follow your mailings through to the bitter end. Track every sale and every return by source to get a true picture of what really works — and what doesn't.

11

CUSTOMER RELATIONS

a. DEVELOPING SOUND CUSTOMER RELATIONS

No matter how successful your direct-mail campaign is, all that success can be sent right down the drain by poor customer relations. You may *get* customers with clever copy and unbeatable bargains, but you won't *keep* those customers very long if your processing is slow, your staff is unhelpful, and you gripe and dawdle over returns. This chapter's focus is keeping, rather than merely getting customers.

Your customers are valuable to you. To realize just how valuable, consider Table #1. At the low end, if you lose one customer each week who spends $5 weekly, you are losing $94,900 a year. At the high end... well, you can see for yourself. Suffice it to say that your customers are important.

The American Management Association says that for some United States firms, customer turnover can run as high as 35% a year. Why? Because most companies spend a great deal of time and money trying to get new customers but spend very little to keep the customers they've already earned.

Good customer service may cost money in the short run, but will pay off with substantial long-term benefits — like customer loyalty.

Can you afford to have even one disgruntled customer? Customer relations and customer responsiveness have be-

TABLE #1
THE VALUE OF A CUSTOMER

The Value of a Customer

Do you think that losing one customer wouldn't really hurt your company?
Think again. Below is a chart that shows the annual revenue loss you would
experience if you lose varying numbers of customers spending $x amounts with you
on a weekly basis.

Revenue Spent Per Week

# Customers Lost	$5	$10	$50	$100	$200
1 a day	$94,900	$189,800	$949,000	$1,898,000	$3,796,000
2 a day	189,800	379,600	1,898,000	3,796,000	7,592,000
5 a day	474,500	949,000	4,745,000	9,490,000	18,980,000
10 a day	949,000	1,898,000	9,490,000	18,980,000	37,960,000
20 a day	1,898,000	3,796,000	18,980,000	37,960,000	75,920,000
50 a day	4,745,000	9,490,000	47,450,000	94,900,000	189,800,000
100 a day	9,490,000	18,980,000	94,900,000	189,800,000	379,600,000

come important issues and are commanding more and more attention from every level in every company. Receptionists, managers, or sales representatives, every employee needs to know how to treat customers right.

The really good companies care about their customers (or clients) and want to keep them happy. According to the Strategic Planning Institute in Cambridge, Massachusetts, corporations that pay careful attention to service quality can charge more for their basic products, gain market share faster, and have a better return on sales than companies that don't.

Examples of the lengths these companies will go to maintain a satisfied clientele abound. For instance:

- Paul Hawken, one of the owners of Smith & Hawken, a garden supply company, speaks of "legendary customer service" and sets an example for others — regardless of the business they're in. A customer who lived 1,000 miles from the Smith & Hawken office once called wanting to know how to deal with a wooden garden bench he had damaged during assembly. Hawken called a carpenter friend in the customer's area and had him go over to fix the bench — at no charge to the customer.

- Schwab Verrand is a German mail order company. One of their advertisements reads "If you are more than 222 centimeters tall then we will give you a free jogging suit with your initials on it. If you aren't that tall, then you can buy one for DM 39.90." They received a request from a man who wrote in to ask for a jogging suit for his dog. What did they do? They made it!

Unfortunately, not all companies express this same high level of concern for their customers. Less than half of the consumers surveyed by Cambridge Reports said customer service is as good today as it was in the past. Gallup Poll participants compared the status of current to past customer service more favorably, but a significant majority said that the current level of customer service they receive is unsatisfactory.

Business today is competitive regardless of the field you're in. In the business world, there are primarily three ways to compete — on service, on price, and on quality. We'll assume that you're doing all you can to enhance the quality of your product or service and that your price is on target. That leaves service — an important tool in today's competitive business climate.

You can't afford to create unhappy customers. And, in fact, keeping them happy and, thus, setting yourself apart from your competitors, doesn't have to be a difficult, time-consuming, or expensive proposition.

There are three critical opportunities for you to influence your customer's perception of your company and its products or services. They are —

(a) initial contact,

(b) continuing contact, and

(c) exception service.

b. INITIAL CONTACT — TAKING AND PROCESSING ORDERS

First impressions count. It's as true in the direct mail business as it is when you're going to a job interview or meeting someone for the first time.

What's the first impression that your company makes? Your very first contact with a customer will, no doubt, come when they first receive one of your mailings. That's why it's so important that you carefully consider the impression you want to make when you design and write your mailing pieces and that you are careful to avoid errors, to make it easy to read, easy to understand your offer, and easy to respond.

If your mailing has made a good impression, you will have a chance to reinforce it when a customer makes contact with your company either by phone or by mail to order or inquire.

Orders arrive primarily in two forms: verbally, via phone, and on paper, via mail or fax. We'll take a look at some of the basic considerations for handling each of these formats.

1. Telephone orders

(a) Make it easy

How can your customers get in touch with you? Is it convenient for them? Do you offer a toll-free number? Most direct mail companies do and they find that the minimal expense is well worth it. If you do have toll-free lines, do you have enough lines? Can customers get through to you or do they continually get a busy signal when they try to call?

To save money, many companies offer a toll-free line for ordering and a toll line for other customer calls. You may decide to do this as well. If you do, make sure your customers are familiar with both numbers. If a customer inadvertently calls the toll-free line, train operators to provide them with the toll number in a friendly way. Keep in mind though, that some customers will insist on getting a satisfactory answer from the operator regardless of which line is being called. Prepare your operators for this by cross-training them to handle both orders and customer inquiries.

Make sure that all telephone staff are kept informed about your products, your promotions, and your policies and procedures. There's nothing more frustrating to a customer (and to the person answering the phone!) than to speak with someone who has no idea what the caller is talking about, who can't answer questions, and who seems to know nothing about the product.

The important consideration with phone orders is that you have enough lines and enough operators answering those lines so that customers can get through to you without hassle. Too many busy signals or too much of a delay in getting a call answered, and an order can be lost.

Most companies carefully monitor their call levels to determine staffing requirements. Further, they establish solid guidelines like, "90% of all calls will be answered without a delay and within three rings."

As you measure your call levels, you'll find that you experience many peaks and valleys in phone activity. After a large mailing, for instance, your telephone calls will pick up. When mailing levels are low, call levels will be too. Making use of part-time staff can help you effectively deal with these peaks and valleys so you don't find yourself overstaffed during slow times or understaffed during peak activity.

(b) Make it helpful

Let's assume you have ample lines to serve the needs of your customers. The next thing you need are well-trained personnel handling those incoming calls. Examine your personnel carefully and hire only the best. These are the people who will be dealing most directly with your customers. You want to make sure they have pleasant speaking voices, that they are courteous and knowledgeable about your product line, and that they convey the proper company image.

For direct mail companies, the person on the other end of the phone is your company. With phone-in orders this is possibly the only person your customer will have contact with. With this in mind, are you confident that you have the right person on the other end of the line?

In addition to having the right people, you want to make sure those people have the proper equipment and information to perform their jobs well. They need to have strong product knowledge and access to customer order information so they can answer questions quickly and knowledgeably.

If a customer calls in with a question about a product and the operator responds "I really don't know, I just take orders," what kind of impression does that leave about your company? Give your customer service representatives adequate training, ready access to complete information about products, including availability of those products, and complete information on customer history. When customers call in to ask if a particular item is in stock, your phone representatives should be able to provide an immediate response. When they ask about the attributes of a particular product, they should be able to expect that the person on the phone knows the answer.

Good people, good training, and good equipment are musts. In addition, you need to empower your people so they can perform effectively. Make sure that you give employees the latitude they need to deal effectively with customers on an on-going basis.

At Smith & Hawken, the garden supply company mentioned above, each customer service representative is told the following:

(a) Establish the concept of "legendary service." Take pride in doing customer service well.

(b) You are the customer. Always look at the situation from the customer's perspective.

(c) You are the company. You have the power to act and the company will give you this power.

(d) There is no such thing as taking too much time with the customer. The amount of time you spend should be the amount of time it takes to resolve a situation.

(e) The phone is mightier than the pen. Resolve the situation now, while you are on the phone. Letters (that may never arrive) only allow the customer to stew.

(c) Make it efficient

To make internal processing as efficient as possible, your telephone operators should work with the same order form that your customers are using. They can simply transfer the information they receive over the phone to this form and pass it on to your data entry personnel.

If you have many different order forms circulating among your prospects, you might want to consider the development of a standard telephone order form that operators can use.

The speed with which you process orders will be an important element of your initial contact. Customers have an expectation that if they place an order one week, their product(s) will be in their hands the following week. Can you meet these expectations?

2. Mail and fax orders

If you use a post office box, be aware that to some people this can suggest "fly-by-night" operations. Anyone can rent a post office box, collect orders and money, and leave town. If you do use a P.O. box (and, again, most direct mailers do), use a street address as well to show that you do have a solid base of operation. For instance:

XYZ Company
1234 Solid Road
PO Box 2541
Anytown, USA 00000

While fax orders are becoming more and more common, the bulk of your orders will still come through the mail. Written orders should be processed as quickly as phone orders. Don't allow mail to sit around unopened for even a short period of time.

In *Fenvessy on Fulfillment*, the following steps are provided for processing mail. Fenvessy further advises that these steps should be performed within 24 hours of the receipt of the order:

(a) Remove orders from envelopes.

(b) Sort and batch.

(c) Handle and balance checks and currency.

(d) Obtain credit approval.

(e) Edit and code.

(f) Enter data into computer and control output.

(g) Produce acknowledgements, invoices, shipping directives, and picking lists.

Fax orders and mail orders can be handled by the same process, except that, obviously, fax orders do not need to be removed from envelopes and they do need to be integrated into the general system immediately.

Staff should also be trained to handle order problems. The two most common are —

(a) incomplete information on the order form, and

(b) incorrect dollar amount submitted.

You will need to develop your own methods for dealing with situations like these. When information is incomplete, it's most efficient to call the customer to obtain the missing information. This is why it's so important to request a daytime number where the customer can be reached. Some customers won't supply a phone number because they fear calls from telemarketers. You might consider including a statement on your order form such as "Please include your daytime phone number in case we have questions about your order."

There are a couple of ways you can handle incorrect amounts sent in payment. In the case of an overage, you can either refund the customer or include a "credit" on the invoice. In the case of an underage, you can either contact the customer and request the correct amount before shipment or include an "amount due" on the invoice. Some companies ignore a certain underage in payments submitted. Usually $2 to $5 or 10% of the order is simply absorbed by the company. Again, these are considerations you will have to make provision for in your internal procedures.

c. CONTINUING CONTACT

1. Keeping customers happy

Once you've established a working relationship with your customers, how can you keep them happy? Much of what was discussed above also applies here. Try these tips:

(a) Orders should be delivered within one week of the receipt of order. This time lag should be shorter for phone and fax orders since these customers are obviously signifying a greater urgency than those who mail in their orders.

(b) All customer inquiries should be answered within one calendar week.

(c) Most calls should be answered without a holding delay; most problems should be resolved while the customer is on the line.

(d) Merchandise should be in stock and on hand.

(e) Offer a guarantee. This is an important "risk-reliever" in direct mail. Customers want to know that, if they're not happy with their merchandise, they can return it without hassle for a full refund.

(f) On-line customer information is crucial. When customers take the time out of their busy days to call you, they want to get some answers immediately. They don't want to be told, "I don't have that information. I'll have to check into this and get back to you."

One important area of ongoing customer service is billing. Billing should be handled very carefully and coordinated with the shipment of orders and processing of returns. Customers don't look upon it kindly when they receive a bill (or, worse, a late-payment notice) for a product they've already paid for or one which they've returned.

The key to providing the right level of ongoing service is meeting customer expectations. How do you know what your customers expect? You ask them. Monitor customer satisfaction by including brief questionnaires with orders and ask telephone representatives to solicit feedback over the phone.

These are the areas in which you should be continually striving for customer feedback —

(a) quality of products,

(b) convenience of ordering,

(c) variety and depth of merchandise,

(d) ease of placing orders,

(e) ease of making returns, and

(f) accuracy of orders.

2. Handling returns

No matter how wonderful your product is, there will always be customers who, for one reason or another, decide they don't want it after all. Returns are simply a part of doing business in direct mail (or any other type of business, for that matter). The processing of a return should be handled in such a manner that a negative experience (for your customer) is turned into a positive one. Make it easy to return merchandise — and easy to receive a full refund.

Returns should be processed with the same efficiency that orders are handled. Whether a refund is in order or not, all returns should be acknowledged.

To expedite the returns process and to avoid the problem of receiving returns with no indication of who the buyer was, many companies include return instructions (and even postage-paid return labels!) when orders are shipped. Instruct your employees who receive returned merchandise to check for a return address and/or ordering information and to keep the shipping box with the product until the appropriate data entries can be made.

Most importantly, don't look upon returns as rejections or upon the customers who returned the products as "cads." Often those customers whose negative responses (whether it be a complaint via phone or mail or a product return) are handled cheerfully and quickly become the best customers of all!

d. EXCEPTION SERVICE

Exception service occurs when a customer calls or writes you to say, "I've got a problem." When a customer has a problem, you have a problem. You want to get that customer back on your side as quickly as possible. This is your opportunity to do so.

When a customer takes the time to contact you, especially about a problem, you're being given a special opportunity — the opportunity to leave that customer with a very positive feeling about your company.

According to research done by Technical Assistance Research Programs in Washington, D.C., only 4% of dissatisfied customers let businesses know they are unhappy. And, as if that's not bad enough, these dissatisfied customers will tell 8 to 10 others about their problem. Your task as the owner of a direct-mail company is to view complaints as feedback and ask for more!

That's right. You should attempt to increase the number of customer complaints you receive. Since only 4% of your dissatisfied customers will tell you they're dissatisfied, the other 96% will suffer in silence or express their dissatisfaction with their pocketbooks — pocketbooks that won't open when your brochure comes in the mail.

Consequently, you want to view complaints as feedback and encourage that feedback as a means of improving your products and services. You can encourage feedback by responding positively when you receive it and by encouraging it openly. Instead of the pat, meaningless question, "How did you like the product?" solicit more meaningful responses by asking, "What can we do to improve our product?"

Any unpleasant customer contact should be turned into an opportunity to show that you care and that you want to do a better job next time. Make your entire company accessible to customers — not just the customer service representatives. Consider the impact it can make on a customer to be able to speak with the owner of the company about a complaint. This is not to say that your customer service representatives cannot do a good job of handling negative customer feedback. But you should never feel that it's an imposition on your time to deal with customers yourself as well.

e. TIPS FOR EXCELLENT CUSTOMER SERVICE

How can you keep your customers happy and keep them saying good things about you? You can emphasize service. You can treat your customers and clients with the same respect and courtesy that you'd show to a good friend. And, as long as your attitude is genuine, the results you reap will be positive ones.

What are some things you can do to set yourself apart? There are dozens. Following are just a few that you may be able to put into practice.

1. Offer a good product or service

First and foremost you have to offer a good product or service. If your products don't stand up to the test of time, good service isn't going to help business. And, likewise, no matter how friendly your employees are, customers won't be standing in line to make purchases if your product is faulty.

Good products and services seem to sell themselves. You can tell if your company has a good reputation (or if you do), if a lot of your business is built upon referrals.

2. Sometimes you're the product

When someone knows a lot about you and treats you like an old friend, you will think twice before taking business elsewhere.

- A beautician who always remembers your name, your husband's name, your children (and their ages!) and carries on a continuous friendly discussion with you as she does your hair is one you won't forget.

- A tax preparer who doesn't get down to business until you've discussed how you like the home you bought the previous year, how Junior is doing at college, etc., is almost guaranteed that you'll be back.

- A banker who seems really concerned about you and offers you advice on investments that fit your lifestyle is one you won't want to give up.

Why? Because, in a small way, these people become your friends. And, as we all know, it's very difficult to give up good friendships.

Does it matter that the knowledge these people have of your life may be on 3" x 5" cards they keep in a file or in copies of prior tax statements or in a sophisticated computer file? Not if you don't know about it.

You can create the same type of rapport with your customers, regardless of the type of business you have, by being a good listener, having a good memory, and, yes, even maintaining a "dossier" file of your own! When you do this, you become part of what the customer is buying. You become the product.

3. Keep in touch

You know what happens when you've got an old friend you don't have contact with for a while — you drift apart. The same thing can happen with your customers, unless you make a conscious attempt to keep in touch.

How can you do this? Try —

(a) regular mailings,

(b) customer newsletters, and

(c) special occasion cards and notes.

(a) Regular mailings

Schedule regular mailings to all of your customers — at least once every other month. These mailings could simply be brief letters reminding customers about the value of your service, announcing special sales, or including little informational notes about some aspect of your business.

(b) Customer newsletters

A newsletter offering helpful advice for your customers is another way to keep your name before them and provide a special service at the same time. If you have the budget and the time, a newsletter might be just the option for you. If, however, a newsletter seems too ambitious, you might decide to send out monthly flyers with helpful information included.

(c) Special occasion cards and notes

You know how special you feel when someone remembers your birthday, anniversary, or other important event. Your customers will feel special too. You can maintain a tickler system that helps you to remember these important days and, as they approach, you can mail out a card with a personal note to appropriate clients. It's just one more way to keep your name in front of your customer base.

4. Make your entire staff a part of your customer service program

It's important that every employee that works for you understands the value of your customers or clients and plays a positive role in maintaining their good will. You don't want to have the kind of people who gloat over every opportunity to "screw a customer" (some companies are saddled with this problem).

You need people who revel in being able to provide quality service that will maintain a strong customer base and build solid referrals. How can you do it? By developing a customer-oriented attitude that's felt company-wide. Set an example at the top. The way you speak about customers and clients will have a strong bearing on the attitude exhibited by your staff. Make sure that you treat customers with respect both in their presence and in the presence of your staff. (For more tips about customer service, see *Keeping Customers Happy*, another title in the Self-Counsel Series.)

Establish employee awareness programs that emphasize the importance of your customers. Display posters that encourage sound customer relations. Reward employees who offer exceptional service to customers or who go out of their way to make sure the customer is "always right." In fact, some companies prominently display a sign which reads:

COMPANY RULES

- Rule #1: The customer is always right.

- Rule #2: If the customer is wrong, refer to Rule #1.

A customer-oriented attitude like this one can't go wrong. Here are some additional means companies use to ensure that customer relations is emphasized in their business:

(a) Requiring that each manager call one customer or client each month to ask "How are we doing?"

(b) Including in all job descriptions some type of customer relations duties.

(c) Inviting regular customers or clients in for "focus groups" to gather their ideas and encourage their feedback.

(d) Following up on problem situations. If a customer has complained about your product or service, call back a few weeks later to make sure the problem has been resolved to his or her satisfaction.

(e) Following up on calls made by your sales personnel or customer relations staff. Check with the customer to make sure that everything was handled to their satisfaction and that your representative was friendly and helpful. Ask for feedback on how you could further improve your customer relations in the future.

(f) Sponsoring special "customer awareness weeks," when everyone in the company is encouraged to make contact with a customer.

f. HANDLING PROBLEMS

There are a number of commonly occurring but sticky situations that direct mailers must deal with. Following are three of these with suggestions on how to deal with each.

1. The wrong price was listed in your mailing

One proactive step you can take to deal with this problem is to include a disclaimer in all of your mailings. But, even with such a disclaimer, problems can develop. The most common action used by direct mailers when the price difference is substantial enough that it cannot be honored, is to simply notify the customer that the price was listed incorrectly and give them the option of canceling their order. At the same time, many companies enclose a certificate good for a discount off future orders.

2. The product the customer ordered is on back-order status

This is bound to happen on occasion and you need to be prepared to deal with the situation. If you will be able to fill the order within the specified delivery time (or the 30-day FTC requirement), you need do nothing. If, however, the delay will be longer, the customer must be notified.

You may wish to use a form letter for this purpose. Form letters are a time-saving and money-saving device frequently used by direct mailers for customer service. Form letters can take the form of correspondence or actual forms where your personnel check off the appropriate space (e.g., "your refund is enclosed"). There are a number of situations where you might choose to use form letters to save time, including "Temporarily out of stock," "Your refund enclosed," "Please remit…" etc.

Many companies send a discount certificate with the backorder acknowledgment as a means of apologizing for the inconvenience and maintaining good customer relations.

3. You're understaffed and the phone lines are ringing off the hook

This can also happen when you're fully staffed, for example, if a mailing worked better than you anticipated and customers are calling frantically.

While this certainly isn't a bad situation to be in, you want to maintain a high level of service and you don't want customers to have their calls go unanswered.

The best way to deal with this problem is to train other personnel in your company to serve as back-up in these situations. Many companies train everyone from the receptionist to the CEO to take phone orders.

g. CONCLUSION

Never forget that every message that leaves your company, whether it's over the phone, in a letter, or in an advertisement or brochure, is a corporate message. The job of good customer relations begins with employee education. Your employees have to fully understand your corporate philosophy. Lack of training, stressful job conditions, poor systems, and unrealistic policies can all cause employees to develop bad attitudes, and these bad attitudes are often directed at the customer.

Whenever you're dealing with a customer or client, you're not in it for the short haul — you're in it for the long run. And you'll stay in the running if you understand the importance of customer relations and always remember that little things mean a lot.

RECOMMENDED RESOURCES

a. ASSOCIATIONS

Direct Marketing Association
6 East 43rd St.
New York, NY
10017

Canadian Direct Marketing Association
1 Concorde Gate, Suite 607
Don Mills, Ont.
M3C 3N6

b. LIST COMPANIES

Hugo Dunhill, a list company in New York, offers free brochures — "How to Prepare a Direct Mail Brochure That Sells"
and "How to Prepare an Effective Direct Mail Letter" — to
anyone who does direct mail and buys lists.

Call 1-800-223-6454 or write to:
Hugo Dunhill Mailing Lists, Inc.,
630 Third Ave.
New York, NY 10017.